At David C Cook, we equip the local church around the corner and around the globe to make disciples. Come see how we are working together—go to **www.davidccook.org**. Thank you!

transforming lives together

What people are saying about …

WRETCHED SAINTS

"In *Wretched Saints*, Noel Jesse Heikkinen does a fine job dispelling the myth that Christianity is chiefly a religion of judgment, scolding, and separation. Instead, he paints a compelling picture of how awareness and admission of sin become a pathway to enjoying the grace and love of God. For Jesus did not come for the healthy but for the sick, He did not come for the righteous but for sinners, and where sin abounds, grace abounds all the more! Take a risk. Read this book and see if perhaps you've misunderstood Christianity all along."

Scott Sauls, senior pastor of Christ Presbyterian Church, Nashville, and author of *Befriend* and *Irresistible Faith*

"In *Wretched Saints*, my pastor Noel lays out the wonderfully paradoxical truth of the gospel. You are both a sinner, saved by God's relentless grace, and a saint, covered completely by the cross. In the chapters of this game-changing book, you will unearth practical truths to help you stop striving—yet simultaneously keep growing—as you rest in God's love and allow Jesus to do the heavy lifting, making you more like Him."

Karen Ehman, *New York Times* bestselling author of *Keep It Shut*, Proverbs 31 Ministries speaker, and Bible teacher

"It's more than a coincidence that the words *wretch* and *retch* are so similar. So much of what Heikkinen covers in this book are the aspects of our own sinful nature and struggles that make us feel like puking. But he does a brilliant, pastoral job of not wallowing in that mess and, instead, giving hope from the depths of God's grace. This book is a great help to people like me, who have been professing Christians for most of our lives and struggle with guilt and inadequacy. And it is a great help to new believers who are figuring out just how hard it is to pursue holiness."

Barnabas Piper, author and podcaster

"With refreshing transparency and deeply biblical truth, Pastor Noel Heikkinen will reconstruct the faith you once had when you first believed that Jesus loved you.… It's time to stop listening to the lies that point you toward introspection and the never-ending search for self-approval and to rest, really rest, in Christ's declaration, 'It is finished!' I love this book. Pick it up and let its message liberate your soul."

Elyse Fitzpatrick, author of *Finding the Love of Jesus from Genesis to Revelation*

"I loved *Wretched Saints*! It's the kind of book one doesn't read just once. The lies we've believed are too ingrained and the gospel so radical that we have to be reminded repeatedly about the truth of our faith. Noel Heikkinen has done that with great skill, humor, and truth. Read this book, keep it in your library, and read it again and again."

Steve Brown, author, seminary professor, and broadcaster, Key Life Network (www.keylife.org)

"If *tired* and *overwhelmed* are words that come to mind when you think about your Christian life, then let Noel help you to be overwhelmed once again by God's tireless grace for 'wretched saints' like us."

Thomas J. Terry, executive director of Humble Beast, and lead pastor of Trinity Church of Portland

"Martin Luther said that justification by faith must be continually in our ears or else we will doubt and forget it. *Wretched Saints* more than rises to the challenge, resounding with the good news that God meets us in our mess with His saving grace and that His love isn't changing, even though we continually second-guess it. What a deeply engaging and ever-urgent reminder of the gospel."

David Zahl, director of Mockingbird Ministries, editor-in-chief of *Mockingbird* (blog), and on staff at Christ Episcopal Church

"Have you ever felt like it's only a matter of time before people find out? Before they find out about your imperfections, sins, lies, and hypocrisy? If so, then you've probably also felt the simultaneous tension of wanting to leave that all behind and walk in freedom. In *Wretched Saints*, my friend Noel will help you identify the lies that are holding you back so that you can embrace the truth that will lead you into a life of freedom."

Daniel Im, author of *No Silver Bullets*, teaching pastor, and director of Church Multiplication, LifeWay

"Some writers provide well-argued, biblical foundations for living under grace. Others show how that kind of life might be lived. Noel excels at doing both in this book. It's wise, insightful, massively encouraging, and highly recommended."

Joel Virgo, pastor at Emmanuel, Brighton, UK

"When it comes to living life in light of God's grace and mercy, too many Jesus followers 'believe' the theology but never experience the reality. In *Wretched Saints*, Noel Heikkinen shines a bright light on the truth of God's declarations about what He's done and who we've become in Christ."

Larry Osborne, pastor at North Coast Church, and author

"I love books that draw attention to the nature of grace. I love it even more when a book brings grace to the places we actually live. If you have felt the tension of being a sinner and being justified by God at the same time but you don't know how to live in the tension, this book is for you. I can't wait to get *Wretched Saints* into the hands of the people of the church I pastor."

Harvey Turner, founder of Living Stones Churches, pastor of Living Stones, Reno, Acts 29 US West Leadership Team

NOEL JESSE HEIKKINEN

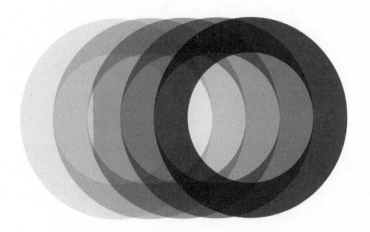

WRETCHED
SAINTS

TRANSFORMED BY THE
RELENTLESS GRACE OF GOD

DAVID C COOK

transforming lives together

WRETCHED SAINTS
Published by David C Cook
4050 Lee Vance Drive
Colorado Springs, CO 80918 U.S.A.

Integrity Music Limited, a Division of David C Cook
Eastbourne, East Sussex BN23 6NT, England

The graphic circle C logo is a registered trademark of David C Cook.

The website addresses recommended throughout this book are offered as a
resource to you. These websites are not intended in any way to be or imply an
endorsement on the part of David C Cook, nor do we vouch for their content.

Details in some stories have been changed to protect
the identities of the persons involved.

Bible credits are listed at the back of the book.
The author has added italics to Scripture quotations for emphasis.

LCCN 2018952799
ISBN 978-1-4347-0996-7
eISBN 978-0-8307-7715-0

Published in association with the literary agency of Mark
Sweeney & Associates, Naples, FL 34113.

The Team: Laura Derico, Jeff Gerke, Amy Konyndyk, Jack Campbell, Susan Murdock
Cover Design: Nick Lee
Cover Photo: Getty Images

Printed in the United States of America
First Edition 2019

1 2 3 4 5 6 7 8 9 10

111618

To everyone who has offered me a glimpse
of the relentless grace of God.
Thank you.

To everyone whom I have failed to offer
even an inkling of the same grace.
I'm sorry.

CONTENTS

ACKNOWLEDGMENTS

You really can't write a book on grace without thanking the people who have taught you about it and modeled it for you.

To my wife (Grace), my kids (Emma, Jesse, Ethan, and Cole), and the people who won't ever leave my house so you have become family (Yoshi and Cameron). You guys see my desperate need for grace more than anyone else, and God has used you as a means of grace in my life.

To a bunch of grace-oozing people who know me well and a bunch of people I have never met (and yet you inspire and teach me anyway), thanks. This growing list includes Timothy Peng, Brian Lowe, the Riverview pastors, David Zahl, Larry Osborne, Martin Luther, Mom, Dad, Steve Brown, Rachael Denhollander,

Paul Tripp, Matt Davis, Steve Treichler, Elyse Fitzpatrick, Philip Yancey, Mark Bowen, and Brennan Manning, to name a few.

To the David C Cook team. I know a lot of you signed on to this project because you believed in me and that was a stunning act of grace. A special shout-out goes to Jeff Gerke, who helped me find my voice and gain clarity on what God was teaching me in a crucial season of my life.

INTRODUCTION

THE ENDLESS QUEST TO FIX A NONEXISTENT PROBLEM

A few years ago, I was in the market for a used car. Like any car shopper, I had my list of nonnegotiables. And, like any middle-aged man, one of my nonnegotiables was *fun*.

I scoured through online listings from around the country with my list in hand and found the perfect car. The only problem was that it was in New York and I lived in Michigan. But I *knew* this was the car. It had everything I wanted: sweet styling, leather seats, a sunroof, a six-speed manual transmission, twin-turbo engine. In other words, it was *fun*.

After a bit of negotiation on price and a few video tours around the car, I bought it and had my new baby shipped to my office when I was out of town. John, my "car guy" friend, met the delivery to make sure everything was kosher. After he finished his inspection, he gave me a call.

"The check-engine light is on."

"What do you mean it's on? It was fine a couple days ago when the guy gave me the video tour."

"Do you want me to check the codes?"

"Of course."

A few minutes later, John called me back with the good news. The code was from a faulty sensor and it was an easy fix. We threw a new sensor in there, and just like that, the warning light went away.

Whew.

I have to tell you, that sensor sent fear running through me. Had I made a stupid decision to buy the car sight unseen? Had I been duped? Was this a lemon?

But no, it was just a faulty sensor. False alarm. Much ado about nothing.

A few weeks later, the light came back on. Again, the anxiety shot through me. We checked the code again. Same thing. *A bad sensor.*

Whew again!

The thing was, the car drove fine. More than fine, really. This truly was the most fun car I had ever owned. I grinned from ear to ear every single minute I drove it.

That was, until I would glance down at the check-engine light that continued to turn on and off, seemingly with a mind of its own. I took the car to my mechanic over and over, and there was never anything wrong. Except the sensors. It wasn't just one sensor that was bad, either. It was one faulty sensor after another. One time, a sensor actually blew up as I was driving down the street! Smoke, along with the smell of burning oil and rubber, poured out from under the hood. I thought for sure my engine was toast that time.

Nope, just the sensor.

The sad thing was, I started changing my behavior based on what I knew to be false information. I began to baby the car. I drove it with less passion and more care. I worried that maybe the way I flew through the gears or pushed the RPMs when accelerating was the real problem. Maybe the sensors were really telling me the truth, despite the lack of any evidence to support that conclusion.

Eventually, I couldn't take it anymore. The sight of the warning light was "driving" me to distraction. So I sold the best car I'd ever had.

Now I drive a decidedly less fun, more practical car from a company with a reputation for reliability.

It's fine, I guess. But I don't smile when I drive it.

I've learned that I'm not the only one duped into making a rash decision by a false sensor. Turns out, it happens all the time.

THE *ALLEGEDLY* LEAKY OIL PAN OF GOD'S LOVE

My on-again, off-again love affair with an amazing car with a faulty sensor is a picture of my spiritual life. Perhaps you can see something of yourself in it as well.

I'm a Christian—a pastor, even—and wholeheartedly believe in Jesus and all His works, grace, and promises. But as I'm cruising along in my life, it feels like something important is leaking out.

I don't know about you, but I can almost never shake the feeling that something has gone haywire. Maybe I've sinned too much or I haven't mastered spiritual disciplines enough or I'm just not quite up to snuff in God's eyes. And now I have this sinking suspicion that God's mad at me or that I'm in the doghouse or that He's finally figured out what a lost cause I am.

It sounds silly to write it out like that. Of course He's not mad. His grace covers me permanently. My sins, all of which Jesus paid for on the cross, were all in the future as He sacrificed Himself. So why do I *feel* like His atonement paid for all my sins before I came to Him (which were in the future as He hung on the cross) but any sins I commit after salvation (also in the future as He hung on the cross) are not covered? Or maybe all my sins up to today were covered, but midnight marked the dividing line, and now I need to earn my way back into His favor.

Stupid. False. Crazy.

Sometimes I act like I think I've outrun Christ's forgiveness, dumb as that sounds. I know in my head that I could never out-sin His atonement—and I would tell *you* that about yourself until I was blue in the face—but in the day-to-day reality of my Christian walk, I think differently. I have this nagging feeling that I've finally sinned too much and I'd better do some good deeds or make some sacrifice or get people to approve of me so I can feel (or fool people) that I'm in right relationship with God.

Seriously, would I be such a total screw-up if I were really walking with God? The Bible says I'm a saint (Romans 1:6–7), but I don't think anyone who *really* knows me would look at my life and confirm, "Yup, that guy is a saint."

I guess that's why I keep feeling that God's love leaks out of me. Sure, I confess my sins and work to make restitution and change my behavior, but the sins continue. No wonder it feels like He's unhappy with me. Who wouldn't be? No wonder I cling to all the songs we sing at church about how much God loves me ... because I need to keep hearing that it's true.

I wish I could see your face right now to measure your reaction. I wish I could ask you (and hear your reply) if you could relate to what I'm saying. I'm guessing you can relate, or else you'll probably put the book down soon.

This is a book for saints, for sure, but *Wretched Saints*. Saints—in the sense of believers in Jesus Christ—who don't have it together and who, despite so much effort spent trying not to, continue to sin. And feel wretched about it. They feel that they've got a leaky oil pan of God's love.

FAULTY ENGINE LIGHTS

What if I were to tell you that you don't have a leaky "God's love pan" at all? What if I told you that God's love is permanently full in the Christian's life and is hermetically sealed, a closed system that is not capable, not with any tool or disaster or tinkering, of ever being opened or of leaking?

We think the problem is that God's love and approval and affection for us leak out and have to be continually topped off. But that's not your problem at all because it's not even true.

What then are we to say about these things? If God is for us, who is against us? He did not even spare his own Son but offered him up for us all. How will he not also with him grant us everything? Who can bring an accusation against God's elect? God is the one who justifies. Who is the one who condemns? Christ Jesus is the one who died, but even more, has been raised; he also is at the right hand of God and intercedes for us. Who can separate us from the love of Christ? Can affliction or distress or persecution or famine or nakedness or danger or sword? …

No, in all these things we are more than conquerors through him who loved us. For I am persuaded that neither death nor life, nor angels nor rulers, nor things present nor things to come, nor powers, nor height nor depth, nor any other created thing will be able to separate us from the love of God that is in Christ Jesus our Lord. (Romans 8:31–35, 37–39 CSB)

There is no leak. There can't be a leak of God's love because nothing in this universe can cause a leak. Not you, not Satan, nothing. The problem isn't that God's acceptance of you leaks away; it's that you've got a faulty sensor.

The engine is fine. Nothing is wrong. Nothing is leaking. But something is telling you that there's a problem. And it's such a scary, compelling warning light that you've done what anyone else in your situation would've done: you've believed it.

And if you're like every other Christian I know, you've got *several* faulty sensors, all or most of which you've believed.

Faulty sensors can make you do really dumb things and can leave you absolutely crippled. Absolutely wretched.

In these pages, I'm going to show you how to spot faulty sensors, remove them altogether, and leave your "engine" free to roar down the open highway of the Christian life, living the way it was meant to be lived. You've believed a lie—several, probably—but you're actually just fine in God's eyes. Even if you've got sin that needs to be cleaned up (which I'm sure you do, if you're like me), you can *know* that you haven't lost God's love and you don't need to earn it back. You never lost it. You can't lose it. You don't leak.

The most serious false leak a Christian can believe is the one that results in us doubting God's love for us again and again. That's the one that could blow up and send smoke billowing out from under the hood of your life. It's a lie straight from hell, but it has the power to leave you despairing and miserable. So it definitely has to go.

We're wretched saints, but we're still saints. We're often disobedient children of God, but we're still His children. Our measuring sticks, and the measuring sticks of those around us, are not the same ones God uses. The diagnostics God performs on us are not the diagnostics the world uses. As far as He's concerned, you and I are right on schedule. We are being sanctified. We are being transformed by the radical grace of God, whether we *feel* it or not.

In time, I pray you'll come to see that you don't have to worry about the faulty sensors that are telling you God's love for you has expired. We'll take care of that problem and show you how to spot false readings yourself. Not by assuring you in a hundred different ways that God does still love you. Nope. That's a useless exercise. The system in question is sealed and doesn't need fixing.

The solution to the problem that you don't feel God's love isn't to give you more happy feelings and reminders about His love … but to take away the voices saying His love might leak away. The solution is to remove the faulty sensors.

Then your "car" will run fine. Then you'll operate in the truth and get beyond the roadblocks of trying to keep filling or repairing a leaky engine that isn't really leaking and move into the works Christ has prepared beforehand and crafted for you to accomplish (Ephesians 2:10).

Let's explore how.

CHAPTER 1

WRETCHED SAINTS ARE WE

SILENCING SATAN'S CONDEMNING JACKHAMMER

I have a unique vantage point as a preacher. Weekly, I stand onstage and look at you (or a rough approximation of you) as you look at me. I get the impression that sometimes you forget that I can see you, but oh yes, I see you.

I see all of you.

I see the teenage boy trying to cop a feel with his girlfriend in the front row. I see the puffy red eyes of the woman who undoubtedly fought with her husband (he's the guy with the steely stare sitting next to her) all the way to church. I see the tired mom and the bored son. I see the faithful Bible studier and the hungover college student. I see the soccer moms and investment bankers and small-business owners and lawyers and assembly line workers ... and you are all looking at me.

Crap.

What am I doing up here?

Don't they know I'm a fraud? Don't they know I've got every bit as much sin in me as they do—and lots of the time, even more than they do? Why should they listen to me?

When everyone walks out of this place today, will any of what I say or do make even the tiniest bit of difference? Will the transformative message of the gospel of Jesus penetrate those inky black parts of their souls ... or is this just a mediocre way for all of us to kill an hour?

I'm asking this not just for you, but for me too. Will the gospel penetrate *my* inky black parts?

Double crap.

I used to think this way all the time, but more and more God is changing my perspective. Now I understand that all the inky black parts were melted beneath the extreme light of Christ's forgiveness when I came to Him in salvation.

Oh, I still sin. Much more than I'd like to admit. But not because I have inky black corners of my soul that God's holiness hasn't penetrated. His Spirit is very thorough. I still sin because:

> 1. I have a sinful nature—so, as long as I live in this world, I can't possibly be perfectly sinless (Ecclesiastes 7:20; Romans 7:15–25; 1 John 1:8);

2. I live in a fallen world that sings siren songs of seduction to that sinful nature (1 Corinthians 10:13; 1 Peter 5:8–9; 1 John 2:15–17); and

3. I believe lies (faulty sensors) that cause me to act as if certain things are true about me that are not true in the least (Proverbs 3:5–6; John 8:44; Colossians 2:8).

We can't do much about items one or two. For us humans, life on earth comes with a sinful nature, and that sinful nature is mightily drawn to "the worries of this age, the deceitfulness of wealth, and the desires for other things" (Mark 4:19 CSB). We can and should do whatever we can to put those things to death, but they represent a struggle we're going to have for life.

Item number three, though … Ah, item three.

WHY WE THINK GOD'S LOVE LEAKS AWAY

I was talking with a friend recently who would probably rank her identity as mother first and lesbian second. She told me that she and her wife had recently been oscillating between attending a Unitarian Universalist church and a Buddhist temple because they "enjoy the conversations." I couldn't help but wonder if they were looking for a place to anchor their identities.

It's what we all do, whether we realize it or not. We look at the entire composite of who we are (or at least those parts we can figure out) and we wonder, *Where did this come from? Why am I like this?*

My own identity is anchored in two paradoxically opposite directions: my sin and my savior.

Yeah, I'm a pastor, but don't let my vocation fool you: I am still a hypocrite—more than I care to admit. It pains me to say it.

The truth of the gospel of Jesus is this: I am nothing more than a wretch ... and yet so much more than a saint. I am a *wretched saint*, and that's exactly what I am supposed to be. No more; no less. That is my identity; it is who I am.

If you are a follower of Jesus, it's your identity too, regardless if you like it.

The problem is that we wrap our heads around all of this only *some of the time*. Most days, we feel like a wretch only. Every once in a while, we feel downright saintly. But we rarely experience the power and grace of bringing those two realities together into one glorious identity.

Take Christopher, for instance. Fresh off a painful divorce with the woman of his dreams, he darkened the door of our church because a friend had told him it was the best thing he could do for his daughter. Turned out, it was the best thing he could do for himself. One service in, and he was hooked on Jesus.

Over the months and years that followed, Chris found ways to sprinkle gospel conversations into his workplace and gym, and it was not uncommon for him to fill a church row with people who were trying to figure out what had so radically changed their friend.

But as the painful memories of his ex-wife faded and he and his daughter settled into their new normal life rhythms, he just, well, drifted away. Sunday mornings became the perfect time to work on his physique instead of his spirit, and his daughter was happy enough to sleep in. Bible reading gave way to social-media surfing, and small-group meetings to channel surfing.

Some people would call Chris a backslider. I call him "normal." I actually find it kind of weird when people *don't* go through this stage.

I have known too many Chrises to call this a fluke.

In so many cases, we Christians can sometimes come to feel that our souls are a leaky bucket and the whole Jesus thing just keeps drip-drip-dripping out.

Growing up in a Christian home, Sarah knew so well what a follower of Jesus was supposed to look like that she unwittingly slipped the mask on each week without missing a beat. It was only when she recognized and made eye contact with *that guy from Tinder* while singing about the blood of Jesus that she noticed the disconnect. Why had she felt the need to find acceptance with him?

Drip.

As Angie looked around the living room at the girls in her Bible study, she thought, *We are in this for life.* That was before her husband lost his job and her best friend stabbed her in the back. What was it about her that always invited betrayal?

Drip.

It can seem like everything about the Christian faith leaks. It's not just the initial excitement of a brand-new worldview (church camp high, anyone?); it's also the feeling of acceptance, the supposedly unconditional love, the immeasurable forgiveness. All of it feels like it leaks away.

It's especially painful when we don't see the change in our own lives that we expect to see. We look at others around us and we are amazed at how perfectly put together their lives are.

Can I let you in on a dirty little secret? Those perfect people around you who seem like they have their life together?

They don't.

But when we believe the lie that they *do*, it makes us feel like there is something wrong with us—something permanently jacked up—that keeps us from being truly worthy of the life they apparently have.

I'm uniquely a loser.

I'm uniquely stupid.

I'm uniquely worthless.

I'm a unique disappointment.

It's a damned lie straight from the pit of hell.

These are lies. We listen to them, and we behave accordingly. But the secret isn't to counter the lies and heap up an even bigger pile of statements, memes, and affirmations that say we *are* worthy of God's love. The secret is to get rid of the lies, because then God takes care of the rest. He's already done so. It's only these lies keeping us from enjoying what He's done.

When you have bad information, bad intel, you make bad decisions.

But in the meantime, we feel we don't have the life we should, and we whip ourselves over it. To combat this spiritual disjoint in our lives, we employ a whole host of foolish strategies. Right at the top of the list is buying a book we think will help (sorry for the ironic disappointment). Try-harder sermons and goofy self-help seminars and intense exercise plans and so-called spiritual disciplines (don't get me started) are also common additions to this list, but none of this stuff works.

Sure, we get a shot of adrenaline or a few good days (or even weeks) from these things. But, like a rubber band stretched to its limit, the inevitable *snap* back to reality really stings. And more of God's love leaks out … or so it seems.

Maybe this is why the apostle Paul screamed at his beloved friends:

> You foolish Galatians! Who has cast a spell on you, before whose eyes Jesus Christ was publicly portrayed as crucified? I only want to learn this from you: Did you receive the Spirit by the works of the law or by believing what you heard? Are you so foolish? After beginning by the Spirit, are you now finishing by the flesh? (Galatians 3:1–3 CSB)

And to his friends in Colossae:

> If you died with Christ to the elements of this
> world, why do you live as if you still belonged
> to the world? Why do you submit to regula-
> tions: "Don't handle, don't taste, don't touch"?
> (Colossians 2:20–21 CSB)

What are you doing? he was saying. *Why are you trying to fix
something that ain't broken?*

You read that correctly: You ain't broken. You are wretched,
but not broken.

You don't leak.

You don't need to earn God's love or earn it back. You don't
need to keep the feeling of His love alive in your heart and mind.
You don't need to prove you are a Christian to yourself or other
people.

As crazy as it sounds, you can actually just live.

You know how it's hard to think when someone else's music
is blasting in your ear or there's a jackhammer pounding away
right outside your window? That's a picture of how Satan makes
the Christian life for believers. He's called "the accuser" for a
reason, you know (Revelation 12:10). He's the master of blasting all the oldies from your life—all your shame, all your false
beliefs about yourself, and those old messages that keep you
handicapped in your life—and he pounds away with the jackhammer of accusation, shame, and fear.

He knows that, if he can keep the noise loud enough and give you a pounding headache, spiritually speaking, you won't think clearly, and you won't be able to even see the reality he sees all too well.

The reality he knows intimately is that you don't have to commit another sin in your life.

Now, don't hear me wrong: I'm not saying you will never commit another sin or even that you can pull off a day without sin. None of us can do that. But if we could perfectly execute the teaching of this book, which we can't, we would be unlikely to sin again.

Because *all sin comes from believing lies about God and ourselves.* Adam and Eve were motoring along fine until the serpent came around and lied to them. They bought it, and *boom* ... here we are.

Satan knows he's defeated (Hebrews 2:14). He knows the love of Christ has *sealed* you up into a perfect system of unleaking permanence (2 Corinthians 1:22; 5:5; Ephesians 1:13–14; 4:30). But you and I don't know that. We've forgotten it or never learned it. So he gives his all to keep us from seeing it. Thus, the noise and the headache.

If your enemy has defeated you utterly, about the only vain hope you have left is to keep everyone else from finding out that the war is over and that you lost. Because if they know, they won't listen to you anymore.

To be brutally honest, Christian friends and pastors haven't always been much help here. And I say that as someone who is both of those things. We want to help. We really, really do. That's why we create programs and classes. It's why we tell you over and over that God loves you. It's why we meet with you and cry with you and yell at you and plead with you. But deep down, it doesn't help much as long as you believe lies about yourself. The answer isn't to hear more about God's love.

The answer is to stop listening to lies from Satan's hate.

CHAPTER 2

FAULTY SENSORS

THE DEADLY COST OF BELIEVING A LIE

False intel, if believed, can have fatal results.

Just after Christmas 2017, Wichita, Kansas, police responded to a 911 call about a man at a certain address who had killed his father, was holding his mother and brother hostage, and was threatening to burn down the house.

The tactical-response team placed a sniper in position and rang the doorbell. A man opened the door, and police told him to raise his hands. He did, but then for some reason he reached for his waistband. The police sniper, thinking he was drawing a weapon—and convinced of how dangerous the suspect was—fired his rifle and killed the man.

Unfortunately, none of the backstory was true.

An online gamer had gotten mad at a fellow gamer over some squabble and had said he was going to "swat" the other one to get back at him. Swatting is making a false 911 call to bring the SWAT team to another person's house, supposedly as a prank. In this case, the threatened gamer, probably acting in fear, gave someone else's address instead of his own, and the police responded.

Who knows why Andrew Finch's address was given, since he wasn't even a gamer. Who knows what Finch was reaching for in his waistband. What's certain, and permanent, is that the police were given false information and Andrew Finch, father of two young children, is dead.

Because of false information.

> "That's the information we were working off of," said [Wichita Police Deputy Chief Troy Livingston]. "Our officers came here preparing for a hostage situation. Several got in position. A male came to the front door, and one of our officers discharged his weapon."[1]

If only this were an isolated case of someone acting with a tragic and permanent effect on information that was false and unsubstantiated. The reality is that it's a way of life for all of us.

The shame of it, for a Christian, is that we of all people ought to be walking in the truth, not according to lies.

How many women have aborted their babies based on false-positive test results indicating genetic disorders? How many marriages have ended or never happened because one or both people have given in to fears about how things are "destined" to turn out? How many innocent young men have been gunned down in the street because it appeared they had a gun in their hand when it was only a phone? Countries have gone to war, at least in part, because faulty intelligence announced the presence of weapons of mass destruction in the hands of a sadistic dictator.

It's one thing to know when you're getting false information. In that case, you can usually disregard it and move on. But when you can't tell if the information you're getting is true or false, you can end up believing lies. And acting on them.

When the warning light in your life says *slut* long enough, you begin to believe it.

The same is true with *liar.*

And *manipulator, failure, weakling, idiot, reject, freak, embarrassment, loser, pervert …*

If you stare long enough at the blinking light of a false sensor, you will begin to believe it is true. And when you believe something, you act on it.

If you consider yourself too stupid to ever figure out tough problems, you won't try things that require a sharp brain—even if you could have done them with ease. If you believe you will bungle things if ever given real responsibility, you will avoid taking positions that would give you responsibility, even if, in reality, you would've been perfect for them. Or you will be sure to sabotage yourself in the job, unconsciously, to make your reality line up with your beliefs.

Do you see how acting on a false warning light actually *causes* the lies you believe about yourself to become true? You did that. You made it true because you believed it about yourself.

I once heard a story (on the internet, so it must be true!) about a school in which the paperwork for two groups of students got mixed up. The kids who were supposed to be in the gifted and talented class were placed accidentally in the class for the remedial kids, and vice versa. Tests at the end of the year, when the gaffe was finally realized, showed that the formerly top kids had dropped significantly because of how the teacher had treated them and what the teacher had expected of them. And the "dumb" kids' scores rose dramatically because they were thought of and treated as gifted and talented, and they believed what was said about them.

What we believe about ourselves determines how we behave. We rise or sink to the level we hold to be true of us.

Then it goes another step deeper: you begin to believe that the lie is *the only true thing* about yourself, and you build out your identity accordingly. I've watched people believe their way into being addicts, thieves, adulterers, pedophiles, screw-ups, and more.

It doesn't even matter if something really is or isn't wrong with you. If you believe something is wrong with you, it results in the same actions and outcomes as if something were actually wrong with you. It feels like a destiny you are powerless to resist.

And it's all false.

The truth is that reality is just that: reality. But our minds can cause us to look at reality and see unreality. We are too often faked out by ourselves.

One report says that half of people vividly "remember" events *that never happened.*[2] If you have a memory from when you were younger than two years old, studies show it is probably false.[3] Some researchers are even playing with the idea of implanting false memories as a treatment for anxiety.[4]

Humans, perhaps alone in all creation, have the ability to trust our own faulty sensors to such a degree that we believe unreality to be reality. And when we act on what isn't real, what isn't true, it can lead to disaster.

There isn't a crime, an atrocity, a molestation, a suicide, a self-sabotage, a genocide, a legalism, an arrogance, an adultery, an abuse, an assault, or a staggering fall from grace that doesn't have at its root the belief in something that isn't true. Yet we can believe the lie so utterly that we convince ourselves that what is clearly wrong and sinful is not only okay, but justified and good.

By the way, that's called sin. The Bible calls it exchanging truth for a lie (Romans 1:24–25).

We Christians suffer and sin because we believe lies.

There's someone who lies to us for a living. Jesus talked about him:

> You are of your father the devil, and you want to carry out your father's desires. He was a murderer from the beginning and does not stand in the truth, because there is no truth in him. When he tells a lie, he speaks from his own nature, because he is a liar and the father of lies. Yet because I tell the truth, you do not believe me. (John 8:44–45 CSB)

How did all this start? As I hinted at earlier, we need look no further than our parents Adam and Eve. They lived in a perfect world, untainted by sin. It was all pineapples and nudity every day (the fig leaves are in all the paintings because of sin, by the way). They had perfect fellowship with each other, with creation, and with God.

Until they didn't.

Sin entered the world because Satan introduced a blinking red light on the dashboard of Eve's life:

> "Did God really say, 'You can't eat from any tree in the garden'? ...
>
> "No! You will not die," the serpent said to the woman. "In fact, God knows that when you eat it your eyes will be opened and you will be

like God, knowing good and evil." (Genesis 3:1,
4–5 CSB)

A faulty sensor was introduced into Eve's soul. More than
one, actually.

You can't trust God.

You won't die.

*Everything you are longing for you can have ... if you sin,
that is.*

*God's keeping the best stuff for Himself and leaving you as an
inferior.*

Lies.

Eve believed the lies, and so did her husband. They decided
to act on falsehood as if it were truth. And we know what happened next.

> Then the eyes of both of them were opened,
> and they knew they were naked; so they sewed
> fig leaves together and made coverings for them-
> selves. (Genesis 3:7 CSB)

They believed the lie, they acted on the lie, and then they
continued to act on it by covering up their nakedness. The fig
leaves came after the sin. Despite the fact that God hadn't changed
(James 1:17) and their reality hadn't changed, their beliefs about
themselves and God had changed—for the worse. And when they
acted on the lie, the human race careened into sin.

All based on falsehoods they believed.

We are still careening around today, believing lies about ourselves and God and behaving as if they're true.

That's the bad news.

Here's the good news: You are acting on false information, but that can stop. It's not even your fault that you're hearing these false messages. Satan is screaming them in your ear. The angst you are feeling … it isn't reality and it can end today. I know it really, really *feels* like reality, but stick with me. You are acting on false sensors. The voices in your head that scream, "Unloved! Unaccepted! Unworthy!" are lying to you. They come from the father of lies (John 8:44), the accuser of the brethren (Revelation 12:10).

You have a faulty sensor. That's actually good news, because if you know the problem, you can apply the solution. A faulty sensor needs to be replaced—or just removed.

So how do you know that you have a faulty sensor? It's really simple yet ridiculously hard: *When you believe something about yourself that is contrary to what God says is true about you, you can know your sensor is out of whack.*

That's it.

Feeling worthless? God isn't giving you that message. I don't want to give you a list of scriptures to counter this, though I could. The solution isn't just to counterbalance the lies with a bigger helping of truth (although there will be plenty of that in this book), but to stop listening to the lies in the first place. After that, only the truth will remain, and the truth doesn't leak.

Feeling ugly? God's not telling you that. Where's that message coming from?

Feeling stupid? Unlovable? Unaccepted? Vile? Broken? Second rate?

It's so crazy that we let Satan shout these accusations at us. If you walked up and heard some punk bully saying these things (much less screaming them) to your child, you'd take pretty quick action. But our enemy is invisible, and he can make his voice sound just like our own. Worse, he says our own words back to us. Not the good ones, of course, but the ones that tear us down. So we go on letting them into our ears.

That's why the solution isn't to have someone else standing on the other side of you saying happy sunshine thoughts about God's love for you. That's just more noise, and as soon as you step away from the good messages, the bad ones will still be there to bring you down again. The solution is to get rid of the bad messages coming into your ear.

Truth *is* the solution, but not truth that counters lies one to one. No, if you remove the lies, the truth will become evident, and it doesn't need to be defended, reinforced, or kept fresh in your mind. It's just reality.

Easy, right?

Not even close. As the old saying goes, "If it was easy, everyone would do it."

Let's take a little test. Here's a list of things the Bible says are absolutely true about you if you are a follower of Jesus. You don't make yourself a follower of Jesus by gutting these things up inside of yourself; they are simply true, period.

Ready? If you like writing in books, go ahead and circle the statements you agree with.

- You and God are completely, 100 percent at peace (Romans 5:1; Colossians 1:20).
- You are not condemned no matter what you do (John 3:18; 5:24; Romans 8:1; Colossians 2:13–15; Titus 3:5).
- You are a beloved child of God (Romans 8:15; 2 Corinthians 6:18; Galatians 3:26; 1 John 3:2).
- You are perfect through Jesus (Romans 3:22; 2 Corinthians 5:21; Philippians 3:9; Hebrews 10:14).
- You are a gift God the Father gave Jesus (John 17:6).
- You are a gift God the Father will one day give Himself (Ephesians 1:18).

How many of those do you really believe deep down in your gut? I could keep going, but I think this list will suffice.

These are all true, but our ability to hold on to their truth *about us* leaks out. Not because they become false all of a sudden, but because we haven't removed the bully screaming in our other ear. It's not a question of believing these things in our heart. It's a question of hitting mute on the lies and then going on with life in the presence of only truth.

At this point, you may be tempted to think I am about to spout some psychobabble about the power of positive thinking, but I'm not. My goal in *Wretched Saints* is for you to see reality as it is, to replace the faulty sensor in your life, and to help you live life abundantly. After all, isn't that what Jesus promised?

> I have come so that they may have life and have
> it in abundance. (John 10:10 CSB)

Oh, for that to be true!
It is.

CHAPTER 3

WRETCHED

THE GOOD NEWS STARTS WITH BAD NEWS

*Yea, though I walk through the valley of the shadow of
death, I will fear no evil: for thou art with me.*

Psalm 23:4 KJV

Psalm 23:4 is quoted at so many funerals that we have mistakenly
come to think of it as a *death verse*. But it's not! It's a *life verse*.
Each of us has days that feel like death, days when evil seems to
press in on every side.

All we have to do is take one look at the world around us,
and the devastating effects of sin begin to close in like a coffin.

War, famine, racism, social strife, abuse, neglect, and greed are just the tip of the iceberg of the pain and suffering that planet Earth and her inhabitants encounter daily.

It seems like everything happening in the world is evil and there is a lot to fear. So tragic that every one of those things in the list above is based in people's lies they've believed about themselves and/or God.

It doesn't feel like life should be that way, because it can plausibly be argued that we, at least in the West, are living in the best of times. Advances in medicine have led to longer life spans, the worldwide percentage of people living in abject poverty is at a historic low, and technology is such that we carry our GPS and web-enabled phones around with us all the time and bosses and bill collectors can reach us at any time. (Come to think of it, maybe this *isn't* the best of times.)

Life has never been easier in terms of the grunt work most of us have to do. No more days spent doing laundry or computing large numbers by hand. No more months spent traveling by horse-drawn carriage. No more butchering our own animals for food. No more spending the entire day fishing or hunting to hopefully have enough food for the night. Our technology does so much of this for us, or at least accelerates it. Leaving us free to … fill the time with more stuff!

Nor has a society ever been more "supportive" than ours is today. No child is left behind. Everyone is tolerated. Shaming a person is not allowed (unless that person is a politician). No one need go hungry. No one need sleep on the street. People can identify with any gender (or neither gender) as they please. Want to be vegan or gluten-free? You can shop for that. Want to hear only those people who agree with you? You can tweak social media into an echo chamber.

Facebook is all about being *liked*. No one is allowed to judge anyone else. A man married his smartphone. Internet trolls abound, but are uniformly hated, as are mommy shamers and cyberbullies. And don't even get me started on participation trophies and other empty rewards for nothing.

We just don't want anyone to feel badly about themselves, and the church is marching right in step with the culture. Have you ever heard so many Christian songs or sermons about how much God loves you as we've heard in the last few years? You'd think people were leaking or something.

Despite all these life-changing advances, the world is still a whopping mess.

Go ahead and flip open your favorite news app and see how today's headlines stack up. Odds are good that the news isn't.

And it's not just the big stuff that stings. It's also the general misfortunes and petty annoyances that range from parking tickets to a coworker's halitosis. It's like this world's operating system is glitchy or, worse yet, *programmed* to make us miserable. It's almost as if this world itself was wretched or something (Romans 8:19–23).

As a culture, we have tried to respond to this darkness by saying, "No, no, it's not true. *You* are actually light." But it doesn't ever feel like this answer is true *enough*, because there always seems to be plenty of darkness to counteract the light. Maybe that's because this "truth" is at best shallow and misguided and, worst, only partial.

Let's be honest. If the world hasn't gotten its fill of good feelings about itself with all the self-love going around now, it's just never going to get enough. (I think the same can be said for Christians who still haven't gotten enough God-love yet.)

So if the world doesn't need more reminders of love, what does it need?

It needs wretched saints who fearlessly walk through the valley of the shadow of death because they know God is with them. It needs Christians who live in the pain and sorrow of everyday life with a confidence that comes from outside of them. But until we embrace that we are who and what God wants us to be, it's impossible for us to walk confidently without constantly peering out, around, and inward for the evil we fear is still lurking.

The crazy part is, in order to be set free from this fear of our own wickedness, we need to face it head on.

A WRETCH LIKE ... WHO NOW?

When was the last time you used the word *wretch* in a sentence?

I'm not a psychic, but I'll bet I know when it was: it was at church.

Even if church isn't your thing, I'll bet it was at church (perhaps you were there for a funeral). I can even do one better. I can tell you the sentence you used it in: "Amazing grace, how sweet the sound, that saved a wretch like me."[1]

This famous sentence is stunning because it implies a great deal about ourselves, our spiritual condition, the world around us, and the posture of God. We are wretches, every single one of us. In a world that is addicted to affirmation, I find it rather remarkable that we still sing this song.

But we *are* wretches—beloved wretches, yes, but wretches nonetheless. We have a knowledge of the truth, but so often we walk according to lies. No wonder we're wretched.

I love how, with one breath, Jesus called Peter "Satan" and then, with the next breath, He invited Peter to a very exclusive, private, miraculous event (Matthew 16:23; 17:1–8). Peter (along with James and John) got to see Jesus light up like a firefly, have a conversation with a couple of dead guys, and hear the voice of God declaring Jesus's sonship and authority over all things (Matthew 17).

Why did Peter get to go? Why didn't Jesus make him stay home and do the dishes as penance for being Satan? Was it because earlier in the same chapter he correctly identified Jesus as "the Messiah, the Son of the living God" (Matthew 16:16 CSB)?

No. It's not a system of how many answers you get right compared with how many you get wrong. Peter got to go because that's how Jesus is. He invites us close, not at the pinnacle of our professional discipleship training, when we have our act together; that's not how Jesus rolls. He invites us in the middle of our worst amateur hour. He brings wretched people into the holiest party. He doesn't see us as wretched, after all. So why should we?

Jesus invites us to the party too. He hands us, as He did with Peter, the keys to the kingdom. Unbelievable.

HOLY TOLEDO

When we fail to live like perfect Christians, the false warning lights start flashing and we quickly draw the conclusion that God can never love us or use us for anything meaningful. But nothing could be further from the truth!

Like Peter, we stand in a long line of saints who had to come to terms with their wretchedness in order to be fully used by God. And before we can come to terms with our wretchedness, we have to stand in awe of God's holiness.

Take Isaiah, for instance. The dude has a vision of angels crying out to God:

> Holy, holy, holy is the LORD of hosts;
> the whole earth is full of his glory! (Isaiah 6:3)

Did you see that? "Holy, holy, holy."

The word *holy* has really lost its punch in our culture. When we hear that word, it's almost always attached to something.

"Holy cow."

"Holy moly."

"Holy rising hemlines, Batman!"

Even though these uses of the word are decidedly unholy and flippant, they actually hint at the true meaning of the word. You see, *holy* means "separate." It literally means "cut."

Imagine that sitting in front of you is a huge mass of "normal." Normal feelings, normal relationships, normal batting averages, normal everything. Now imagine that, at the edge of the mass of normal, little pieces have been cut away. These pieces are abnormal, cut off, and separated from that which is normal. They are *holy*.

My wife and I were watching the 2018 Winter Olympics, and we saw Nathan Chen do six quads. Six!

Yeah … that meant nothing to me either.

But people who know figure skating reacted strongly. Michelle Kwan, for instance, tweeted, "Holy Quads."[2] What she was saying was that, in the mass of normal figure skating, Chen was not normal. He was cut off the block, and his quad achievement was *holy*.

When you hear people use the word *holy* in our culture, what they are usually saying is this *thing* they're exclaiming about, whatever it is, isn't normal. It's extreme or unusual. "Holy [whatever]" is a declaration of "I can't believe it! Who is like this?" "Who skates like this?" "Who runs like this?" "Who is beautiful like this?"

In Isaiah, the angels took one look at God and said, "Holy, holy, *holy*!" He is so cut apart from what is normal, He is so separate, that He gets three holies.

In an overly simplistic sense, holiness is the opposite of sin.

We can define sin as any failure to reflect the image of God in nature, attitude, or action. In that way, God is holy. His *nature* is holy (without sin). His *attitude* is holy (without sin). And His *actions* are holy (without sin). He is holy, holy, holy. He is not crooked. He is not evil. He is not broken. He is not distorted. He is holy, holy, holy.

In our world, we get glimmers of holiness that show us the transcendence of God's holiness. When something grabs on to your soul because it stands apart, it's a little bit of holy. Have you ever seen a ridiculously beautiful person or sunset (or strip of bacon), and you just spontaneously declare, "Wow"?

That's a glimmer of holiness.

AT LEAST I'VE GOT THAT GOING FOR ME

A couple of years ago, I got to visit Paris with my daughter. Now there's something you have to know about Emma: she sparkles. Since she was a little girl, she has sparkled both metaphorically and literally. In fact, a couple of weeks ago, I helped her move into her new house (she's not a little girl anymore), and she had glitter all over her legs.

So, there I was in Paris with sparkly Emma, and we were told we really should be standing next to the Eiffel Tower at precisely 10:00 p.m. We made our way over to the landmark a few minutes before the hour. Even at 9:55, it was beautiful—majestic and stately and all lit up against the backdrop of the city. But that was nothing. At precisely 10:00 p.m., it began to sparkle. As did my daughter's face.

She will never forget the sparkle, and I will never forget her face. She is normally a happy, sparkly person, but even for her this was a cut above normal. It was transcendent.

Holiness amazes us like that. It takes us off guard because we aren't used to it. Something that is abnormally gorgeous or breathtaking or stunning tells us a little about who God is. That's part of how creation testifies to God's nature (Romans 1:20). But it's not just the delightfully abnormal that gives us a picture of God's holiness, it's the things that downright terrify as well.

> And the foundations of the thresholds shook at
> the voice of him who called, and the house was
> filled with smoke. (Isaiah 6:4)

When you see something that is so beyond you in its power and might, you can feel frighteningly small. That's what Isaiah felt when he came face to face with God's holiness—he cried out in fear:

> Woe is me! For I am lost; for I am a man of
> unclean lips, and I dwell in the midst of a people
> of unclean lips; for my eyes have seen the King,
> the LORD of hosts! (Isaiah 6:5)

Most of us wouldn't consider ourselves perfect, but we still have something we hold on to in order to justify ourselves. If we believe God's love leaks out of us, we tend to look for ways to feel that we're not complete and we're total rejects who should be cast out from society. So we say, "No, I'm not perfect—but I'm okay because …"

- "At least I'm pretty."
- "At least I'm smart."
- "At least I'm educated."
- "At least I'm artistic."
- "At least I'm unique" (as unique as everyone else).
- "At least I'm Instafamous."

In an attempt to prove our worth and value—because we've believed the lie that we have to do this—we grab on to some specific thing that we think gives us worth and value, and we hold it close and make it the core of our identity.

"I'm okay because at least I'm …"

George Whitefield often declared that, to be saved, we need to repent of two things: our sins and our righteousness. It's obvious why we have to repent of our sins, but it's less obvious why we have to repent of our righteousness. He knew we had to repent of what's not wrong with us too, because otherwise we will think we are saving ourselves.

> What is conversion then? I will not keep you lon-
> ger in suspense, my brethren: man must be a new
> creature, and converted from his own righteous-
> ness to the righteousness of the Lord Jesus Christ.[3]

We need to repent of saying, "I got this. I'm okay because at least I am …"

Tim Keller made an astute observation about this story from Isaiah's life. He pointed out that Isaiah was a prophet, which meant he used his lips every day in service of God. His words, his lips, were the one thing he could hold on to and declare, "I'm okay because at least I have my words!"[4]

But what did Isaiah say about himself when he was faced with how holy, holy, holy God was? "I am a man of unclean lips, and I dwell in the midst of a people of unclean lips" (Isaiah 6:5).

It's easy to see all that is wretched in this world. Many people say we are corrupted by the mere fact that the world is corrupt, and there's probably a nugget of truth to that. But our wretchedness bubbles up from inside ourselves, too, when we believe faulty sensors. Isaiah started with himself and said, "The one area where I can serve as a bastion of righteousness is an example of everyone's sin."

Jesus said it this way:

> "It is not what goes into the mouth that defiles
> a person, but what comes out of the mouth; this

defiles a person." Then the disciples came and said to him, "Do you know that the Pharisees were offended when they heard this saying?" (Matthew 15:11–12)

Jesus's disciples were like, "Hey, Jesus, we aren't sure if You caught it or not, but some of these guys were offended when You said that about the mouth and defiling and everything. Maybe You shouldn't talk like that."

He answered, "Every plant that my heavenly Father has not planted will be rooted up. Let them alone; they are blind guides. And if the blind lead the blind, both will fall into a pit." But Peter said to him, "Explain the parable to us." And he said, "Are you also still without understanding? Do you not see that whatever goes into the mouth passes into the stomach and is expelled? But what comes out of the mouth proceeds from the heart, and this defiles a person. For out of the heart come evil thoughts, murder, adultery, sexual immorality, theft, false witness, slander. These are what defile a person." (Matthew 15:13–20)

Don't point your finger in blame. It's not the corrupt, fallen world making you sin. It's the lust of the flesh and the lies you've believed. Jesus is saying, "Don't you realize that all of your sinful attitudes and actions come from your own sinful heart?" Own it. You are a wretch. So am I.

So was Isaiah.

> Woe is me! For I am lost; for I am a man of unclean lips, and I dwell in the midst of a people of unclean lips; for my eyes have seen the King, the LORD of hosts! (Isaiah 6:5)

Isaiah knew he was sinful because he compared himself to God. Not to others. Not to his own ideals. God. That's the only true way to measure our holiness or wretchedness.

So, if God is holy, holy, holy, what are we to do?

What did Isaiah do? He repented of his sins and his attempts at righteousness. And what did God do in response?

> Then one of the seraphim flew to me, having in his hand a burning coal that he had taken with tongs from the altar. And he touched my mouth and said: "Behold, this has touched your lips; your guilt is taken away, and your sin atoned for." (Isaiah 6:6–7)

In answer to Isaiah's repentance, God took his sin away and atoned for it. In Christ, your guilt is taken away too. Your sin is atoned for. You are made into a saint.

In that moment, Isaiah knew exactly how blown away to be, because for the first time, he saw God's holiness and was able to compare it to his own.

Now, this story is terrific in its own right. We could stop at this point and be amazed. But it doesn't end here!

> And I heard the voice of the Lord saying, "Whom
> shall I send, and who will go for us?" Then I said,
> "Here I am! Send me." (Isaiah 6:8)

Now get this: Isaiah volunteered to be sent even though God had not told him where He wanted to send him. But to Isaiah, it didn't matter. He would do anything for God because he was moved by how much this God loved him. The lies were gone and only the truth of his solidity in God's favor remained.

Before Isaiah could understand how loved he was, he had to understand what a wretch he was. If he had a false view of himself, and thought his life was completely put together, he never would have been able to accept the love of God ... because deep down, he wouldn't have believed he needed it.

In that way, he was just like John.

John's dad was a wealthy slave merchant in the early 1700s. He made his fortune by repeating the same three journeys over and over. He would sail from his home in England to Africa to pick up slaves. From there, he would sail to Jamaica, where he would trade the slaves for sugar and molasses. Then, he would head home to sell the sugar and molasses.

Between the ages of eleven and seventeen, John went on six of these journeys with his dad. And when the time came, John went into the family business and became the captain of his own ship. From his father he had learned to be a harsh taskmaster who was both feared and hated by his men. He played this role so well that, one day when he fell overboard, his crew refused to drop a lifeboat to save him. Rather, they threw a harpoon at him. Luckily for John, they missed, and he grabbed the harpoon and his men dragged him back onboard.

In 1748, on one of these journeys, John stumbled onto a copy of *Imitation of Christ* by Thomas à Kempis, and he began to read it along with a Bible.

This journey had quite an impact, both intellectually and experientially, on young John. As they crossed the Atlantic Ocean, he and his crew hit a storm that threatened to tear the ship to pieces. John, fresh from his time contemplating his eternal soul, cried out to God to save them.

And God did.

This act of grace picked at the edges of John's spirit as he continued to captain his slave ship for six more years. The lies he'd believed began to fall away. On the long journeys to Africa, Jamaica, and England, John taught himself Latin and a smattering of Greek and Hebrew, and he started poring over the Bible in the original languages. This study caused John to draw two deep conclusions: "I am a great sinner, and Christ is a great Saviour."

Moved by this revelation and significant health problems, John gave up his lucrative career as a slave trader and decided to become a pastor. If there were beliefs in his head that he was good for nothing but to be a slaver, they dropped away. Also, for him, it was a penance of sorts because he was haunted by the memory of his captive slaves.

John wasn't, by most contemporary accounts, a very good preacher. But God had changed this man from being a harsh slave trader, who was hated by even his own crew, into a humble and passionate follower of Jesus, who fought tirelessly against the slave trade.

Fully aware of his own sin—and the depth of God's forgiveness—John Newton wrote those famous words.

"Amazing grace, how sweet the sound, that saved a wretch like me."

CHAPTER 4

JUST BELIEVE

IT'S MORE THAN A FEELING

The reason we *try* so hard—the reason we *fail* so often to meet internally and externally imposed standards, the reason we *beat ourselves up* so badly—is that we have a faulty sensor. The sensor blinks, *I'm not supposed to be a wretch anymore; I'm supposed to be a saint.* We are mistakenly under the impression that our sin nature was supposed to have melted away ... or at least be melting away faster than it seems to be. But that's not what the Bible teaches about our Christian life. At least, not precisely.

Let me be as blunt as I can be: You are *exactly* who you are supposed to be, warts and all. You're in process and God's got you on the program He's designed for you. You don't need to take a single step toward Jesus because Jesus has already come all the way to you.

How can this possibly be? Isn't there a ton of Scripture that says we are supposed to be living completely saintly lives or at least *trying* to? You bet there is. Let's look at some of it.

> Do not be conformed to this world, but be transformed by the renewal of your mind, that by testing you may discern what is the will of God, what is good and acceptable and perfect. (Romans 12:2)

> Put to death therefore what is earthly in you: sexual immorality, impurity, passion, evil desire, and covetousness, which is idolatry. On account of these the wrath of God is coming. (Colossians 3:5–6)

> What good is it, my brothers, if someone says he has faith but does not have works? Can that faith save him? (James 2:14)

These are critical verses, and we should never downplay their importance to growth in our Christian faith. At the same time, another theme in Scripture is equally critical to understand.

People who are smarter than me put it this way: imperatives always follow indicatives.

Now, if you are anything like me, you are running through Google a few words right now. Don't worry; I've found an easier way to say it: *as a Christian, what you are called to do always flows from what Jesus has already done.*

It is way too easy to read the Bible and feel condemned. And to be honest, parts of the Bible are *intended* to condemn—they *must* condemn. No one would come to Jesus unless they felt the sting of condemnation that comes from offending a righteous and holy God. But if these parts of the Bible are used to condemn a believer in Jesus, they are being misused (1 Timothy 1:8–11).

For a follower of Jesus, all of Scripture must be read through the gospel lens of what Jesus has already done for us, is continuing to do for us, and will do for us.

Let's take the three examples above.

> Do not be conformed to this world, but be transformed by the renewal of your mind, that by testing you may discern what is the will of God, what is good and acceptable and perfect. (Romans 12:2)

The only way we can resist the allure of the world is through the person and work of Jesus. And don't miss how Paul, the author of Romans, expects us to resist the world: "by the renewal of your mind." Something has to happen in your brain—a renewal has to take place in what you believe. This renewal is possible for the Christian only because of what Christ has done.

> Put to death therefore what is earthly in you: sexual immorality, impurity, passion, evil desire, and covetousness, which is idolatry. On account of these the wrath of God is coming. (Colossians 3:5–6)

These verses also come with a pretty hefty theological on-ramp. In fact, it's good to read the context that precedes them to get a fuller picture.

> So if you have been raised with Christ, seek the things above, where Christ is, seated at the right hand of God. Set your minds on things above, not on earthly things. For you died, and your life is hidden with Christ in God. When Christ, who is your life, appears, then you also will appear with him in glory. (Colossians 3:1–4 CSB)

If you have been raised with Christ (which you have, if you're a Christian), then (1) seek Jesus (who is sitting next to God the Father), and (2) set your mind (there it is again) on Him, confident that you are *hidden with Christ in God*. What we are to do flows out of what Jesus has already done to us. And then put those old passions to death, as the next verses say:

> Put to death therefore what is earthly in you: sexual immorality, impurity, passion, evil desire, and covetousness, which is idolatry. On account of these the wrath of God is coming. (Colossians 3:5–6)

Finally, our third passage:

> What good is it, my brothers, if someone says he has faith but does not have works? Can that faith save him? (James 2:14)

As a Christian, what you are called to do always flows from what Jesus has already done. This verse (which has tripped up a lot of faithful followers of Jesus) seems to be asking for us to prove our faith by doing lots of things. That seems contrary to pretty much all of Christianity, but that is what it appears to be saying. As you might've guessed, this verse has a glorious truth that precedes it and helps us understand it:

> Speak and act as those who are to be judged by the law of freedom. For judgment is without mercy to the one who has not shown mercy. Mercy triumphs over judgment. (James 2:12–13 CSB)

Oh, how I love this one! Speak and act as if you are going to be judged by … what? By freedom and mercy. You know what that means? You can have good works. You will have good works. They will just come out of you because of what God is doing in you.

All too often we let our emotions (fear, anxiety, and even affection and joy) cloud our reading of Scripture. From an emotional standpoint, the commands in Scripture (especially in the New Testament) shouldn't be read as "You should" or "You must," but as "You can" and, if I may be so bold, "You will."

Reading Scripture that way is the key to dealing with the faulty sensor that condemns us or makes us prideful. The remedy for the false stories screamed in our ears is simply this: *believe and focus on what is true.*

That may seem like a ridiculously obvious statement. Duh! Of course I should believe and focus on what is true! But anyone who has walked with Jesus for a long time will tell you that doing so can get harder and harder to do. Life has a way of jacking up what we believe.

Having pastored in the same church for nearly twenty years, seeing the people from the pulpit time after time, I have had the opportunity to watch them age and mature (or sometimes just do one of those things). One truth has become abundantly clear to me: Those who *believe the gospel* the deepest are most acutely aware of their own sin and increasingly gracious toward others when they sin. They act on their belief.

FEEL, THINK, BELIEVE

I've noticed that we use these three words—*feel, think, believe*—too often as if they were interchangeable; though they have wildly different meanings.

"I *feel* like I am going to pass this final exam."

Really? Are you gonna bank your whole GPA on what you feel? Would it be more accurate to say you *think* you will pass? Have you studied?

"I *think* she is cheating on me."

Do you have evidence? If not, at this point that's just a feeling.

Now, *believe* is different. I really appreciate how Tim Challies handles the distinction:

> There is a hierarchy when it comes to the ways we express ourselves and our convictions. There are some things we *believe*, some things we *think*, and some things we *feel*. The terms are hierarchical rather than synonymous and over time we ought to see a progression from feeling to thinking to believing. We should want to elevate more of what we feel into what we think and more of what we think into what we believe.[1]

I think Tim is on to something. If I were to diagram his concept, it would look something like this:

Feelings are the most basic human operating system for decision making—just watch a toddler decide how to respond to bedtime when there are blocks to be played with. All too often adults never grow past this stage, and consequently, their emotions continue to rule over them. Road rage is the emotional result of being cut off in traffic and feeling like you have been disregarded by another driver. Parents yelling at a teenage umpire is the emotional result of feeling like your kid isn't being treated fairly by someone without enough training and experience to officiate a youth baseball game. Overwhelming joy when unboxing a new phone that will be outdated in a matter of months is the emotional result of a feeling that things will fill a void in your life.

A mature (or maturing) person will over time replace these knee-jerk, feelings-based reactions with more thoughtful responses. A terrible driver may be rushing to the hospital to care for a dying loved one. A teenage umpire may be officiating his first game (and your kid isn't Mike Trout, anyway). A new phone is just a tool to make life more efficient and, yeah, a little fun too. A spiritually mature (or maturing) person will take this to the next level, allowing their thoughts to be replaced (or at least trumped) by their beliefs.

While I think Tim's observations are insightful and largely accurate, I would add one little nuance. I think what we truly believe, and therefore act on, flows from both what we think and what we feel. In turn, our beliefs should inform our thoughts, which in time drive our feelings in the same direction. It looks like this:

Some of us are naturally more thinking people, and some of us are more feeling people. Contrary to what both camps would have you believe, neither is superior or a mark of a more mature Christian. They are just different.

My friend Craig is the definition of a thinking person. As is often the case with such people, he is married to a woman who is the definition of a feeling person. They have two boys, and yes, you guessed it, one takes after Dad and one takes after Mom.

One day, his like-minded son asked him a question that had been perplexing him for some time. "Dad, why do Mom and my brother love people?"

Without missing a beat, Craig replied, "That's easy. They love people because they love people. You and I love people because Jesus told us to love people."

Thinking and feeling both are parts of what it means to be human. They can both serve you well. But both can also get out of whack if they are left to their own devices. If our beliefs are solely informed by our feelings and thoughts, our understanding of truth becomes a product of our own life experiences, wiring, and intellect.

That's why it is critical that truth comes from the outside, binding all three together. I would argue that Christian maturity looks like this:

Truth becomes the framework, support system, and ultimate litmus test of what we feel, think, and believe.

Things get tricky when what you believe to be true smacks up against what you feel or think. It's hard to act on a belief that doesn't jibe with everything else inside of you. If you are naturally wired as an "everything is black and white" person, it may be hard to forgive someone who gives you a halfhearted apology, even though you believe you should (Matthew 6:14–15; Luke 17:3–4; Colossians 3:13). When you feel like you are a failure (perhaps through years of experiential conditioning at the hands of ruthless people), it's hard to act on the belief that God accepts and loves you unconditionally.

When your thoughts and feelings drive your belief instead of letting an external truth define it, it makes for a really bumpy ride. This is why Jesus said that what "proceeds from the heart [is what] ... defiles a person. For out of the heart come evil thoughts, murder, adultery, sexual immorality, theft, false witness, slander" (Matthew 15:18–19).

Or to quote Pastor J. D. Greear, "Your heart is an emotional idiot."[2]

I see this principle at work frequently with engaged couples. In their excitement to begin their lives together, they often share a home (complete with a shared bed) before their wedding day because they *feel* God is okay with it. When I point out scripture that says we should reserve sexual expression exclusively for marriage, they counter with their *feelings* of peace on the matter. These feelings act as a trump card to invalidate what the Bible has to say.

It's the same with *thinking* people. Living together before marriage saves money and seems like a logical way of "testing the waters" (even though statistics say the opposite). So, they allow their thoughts to persuade them to *believe* that God wants them to be fiscally responsible, and they move in together during their engagement.

I've seen this principle in play with friends and congregants who are workaholics, lazy, tired of marriage, disrespectful of parents, gay, trans, jealous, bitter, and a whole host of other issues. Because they *feel* or *think* something is true, they act on it as a core *belief* and often even go on a convoluted scripture hunt because everyone can find a verse to warp out of context to support their views.

For Christians, I find that most of these misguided beliefs come in one of two varieties: "I am only a wretch" or "I am only a saint." And that's when things fall apart.

When you deeply believe that you are only a wretch, you think and feel nothing but sorrow, fear, pain, and shame. With that belief comes all the decisions and actions and brokenness that spin out from believing a faulty sensor.

When you deeply believe you are only a saint, you are prideful, arrogant, judgmental, and condemning.

We must believe what the Bible says is true, even (or *especially*) when it disagrees with what we want to believe is true. This idea is so central to our faith that various forms of the word *believe* show up hundreds of times in the Bible, mostly in the New Testament.

In fact, when Jesus launched His public ministry, He did so with the words "The time is fulfilled, and the kingdom of God has come near. Repent and *believe* the good news!" (Mark 1:15 CSB).

The concepts of "repent" and "believe" are necessarily linked. You need to repent (change your mind, turn around) to believe something new—the good news of Jesus.

It's scary to believe something that conflicts with your feelings and thoughts. But we must. If we've got a dashboard light that we know is telling us something false, we have to believe the truth instead. It's hard, though. Maybe that's why Jesus said, "Don't be afraid. Only believe" (Luke 8:50 CSB).

And that's my challenge to you as you read this book: Don't be afraid—only believe! Believe what the Bible says is true about you. Make your feelings and your thoughts line up with that so all three are in alignment.

When you believe that what God says is true about you, you are set free to (1) plumb the depths of your sin without fear of rejection, and (2) soar in the righteousness God gives you without pride.

It's not helpful to think you're not supposed to be a wretch anymore, and it's not helpful to think you're supposed to be a saint all the time. You and I are *wretched saints*. Sometimes we sin and have to get back up, and sometimes we do well and have to watch out for the next sin.

God's love doesn't leak out of you because you sin. As a Christian, what you are called to do always flows from what Jesus has already done. Jesus has paid it all, and you're right where you should be on the sanctification program He's laid out for you.

For the rest of this book, we are going to swirl around what it means to be a wretched saint. Some of this stuff is going to strike you if you're a *thinking* type and some of it will strike you if you're a *feeling* type. All of it is meant to help you believe more that God is transforming you by His relentless grace and that you are right where you are supposed to be.

CHAPTER 5

HIGH STAKES LOST AND FOUND
GOD'S SINGULAR POSTURE OF LOVE

In his seminal work *Ragamuffin Gospel*, Brennan Manning, the late theologian, alcoholic, and addict, reminds us that God "has a single relentless stance toward us: He loves us."[1]

A single relentless stance.

Let that get under your skin. Even though you are a wretch, God's singular posture toward you is one of love. I don't say this by way of an affirmation to help keep your love tank topped off but to describe what the reality is. When the faulty sensor is removed, you can see that this reality has never changed, and never will.

We can see this perhaps no more vividly than in the most famous of Jesus's parables.

> All the tax collectors and sinners were approaching to listen to him. (Luke 15:1 CSB)

Do you see how stunning this is? Let me point out one word: "all." Now go back and read that verse again.

All the sinners were approaching Jesus to listen to Him. There was something about Jesus that was like a magnet for those who were aware they were steeped in sin. They wanted to know what He had to say. They recognized that, when they were with Him, it was as if their sin wasn't what defined them. While their sin, at least as the Pharisees identified it, was great, Jesus acted like it wasn't even there. Like reality in God's knowledge was different from how people saw it.

Another group of sinners (who didn't know or admit their sin) didn't like this one bit:

> And the Pharisees and scribes were complaining, "This man welcomes sinners and eats with them." (Luke 15:2 CSB)

The Pharisees could not believe that any God-fearing teacher would welcome sinners into his presence, let alone eat with them.

Think about the kind of people you would (and more importantly, would *not*) invite over to your house for a party.

For a meal. To spend the night. The best way to know the type of people you would invite over is by looking at your calendar over the last year and seeing who you *did* invite over. How does that invitation list look?

The biblical word for *hospitality* literally means "lover of strangers." If you think you are being hospitable, ask yourself who you invite over. Family? Friends? Neighbors? Who else?

Jesus didn't have a house, so He didn't invite people over much. He actually did something more radical: He went *to them*. He crossed to the wrong side of the tracks and He accepted the hospitality of hookers and drunks and taxmen. He ate with them, even as they ate too much, and He drank with them, even as they drank too much (Matthew 11:19).

Eating with someone, especially in their home, is an intimate thing. You can see what they value by looking at what the fridge magnets are displaying. You can see how well they clean and if they are neat freaks.

How scandalous that Jesus would offer such intimate contact to the worst people the posh religious leaders of the day could imagine. (Hmm, who would be on that list today?)

Jesus responded to their indignation in one of His favorite ways … with a story. Three of them, in fact.

> So he told them this parable: "What man among you, who has a hundred sheep and loses one of them, does not leave the ninety-nine in the open field and go after the lost one until he finds it?

> When he has found it, he joyfully puts it on his
> shoulders, and coming home, he calls his friends
> and neighbors together, saying to them, 'Rejoice
> with me, because I have found my lost sheep!' I
> tell you, in the same way, there will be more joy
> in heaven over one sinner who repents than over
> ninety-nine righteous people who don't need
> repentance." (Luke 15:3–7 CSB)

If I'm brutally honest, I really don't get this parable. It makes zero sense to me. What kind of manager leaves behind ninety-nine percent of his inventory to chase down one percent? An irresponsible manager who is bad at taking care of his investments, is all I can think of. Seriously, what if he loses another sheep or two—or seventeen—while he is out looking for the one that got away? Ludicrous.

But that's precisely the point: God's economy is so much different from ours. Investments be damned. It's the lost *one* that matters to Him, so the shepherd in the story goes on a dangerous mission to find the missing sheep. And when he finds the lost one, he throws a huge party.

Personally, I wonder if lamb was on the menu.

(Too soon?)

Okay, moving on …

> Or what woman who has ten silver coins, if she
> loses one coin, does not light a lamp, sweep

the house, and search carefully until she finds it? When she finds it, she calls her friends and neighbors together, saying, "Rejoice with me, because I have found the silver coin I lost!" I tell you, in the same way, there is joy in the presence of God's angels over one sinner who repents. (Luke 15:8–10 CSB)

Okay, I get this one a little bit more, but mostly because I can't find my Kindle. I spent the better part of the morning on the day I wrote this tearing my house apart. Then I completely emptied everything out of my car. Then I called every restaurant and coffee shop I'd visited in the last week. Nada. I have this vague recollection of setting it down somewhere and thinking, *That's a stupid place to set that down. You'd better remember where it is.* Nope. I do not remember. Ugh.

It's just a Kindle, but I feel like I have lost everything! It syncs online, though, so I really haven't lost all that much. I mean, at least it's not my phone. Oh, man, if I lost that …! So I understand the whole frustration-at-looking-for-something idea Jesus is getting at.

Still, I'm not sure I can think of a single possession I could lose that would merit throwing a party when I found it. It's just stuff. An inheritance check I'd thought lost, maybe. For some people, maybe a precious family pet. But a thing?

Perhaps that's why Jesus's third story strikes us more than the other two. Because this time it's not a sheep or a coin—it's a kid, and I have four of those. Read this through and try to make it as fresh as you can. Maybe think of your own children if you have some.

He also said: "A man had two sons. The younger of them said to his father, 'Father, give me the share of the estate I have coming to me.' So he distributed the assets to them. Not many days later, the younger son gathered together all he had and traveled to a distant country, where he squandered his estate in foolish living. After he had spent everything, a severe famine struck that country, and he had nothing. Then he went to work for one of the citizens of that country, who sent him into his fields to feed pigs. He longed to eat his fill from the pods that the pigs were eating, but no one would give him anything. When he came to his senses, he said, 'How many of my father's hired workers have more than enough food, and here I am dying of hunger! I'll get up, go to my father, and say to him, "Father, I have sinned against heaven and in your sight. I'm no longer worthy to be called your son. Make me like one of your hired workers.'" So he got up and went to his father. But while the son was still a long way off, his father saw him and was filled with compassion. He ran, threw his arms around his neck, and kissed him. The son said to him, 'Father, I have sinned against heaven and in your sight. I'm no longer worthy to be called your son.'

"But the father told his servants, 'Quick! Bring out the best robe and put it on him; put a ring on his finger and sandals on his feet. Then bring the fattened calf and slaughter it, and let's celebrate with a feast, because this son of mine was dead and is alive again; he was lost and is found!' So they began to celebrate." (Luke 15:11–24 CSB)

What an incredible story. It's clear to me why this is arguably the most famous story in the Bible.

With this third parable told, presumably, in one sitting with the other two, the whole lost-found-party rhythm seems to make sense. Lost sheep/coin/son is found and returned to its place, and then … celebration. Of course, any good dad would be excited to see his son come home. Of course, he would wait, yearning for his return.

The beauty of this story, and perhaps a reason it resonates with humans across centuries and continents, is that the father is not waiting there eager to scold or punish his kid. He is waiting to embrace him. This parable grabs our hearts because either we have a dad like that or we have always wanted one like that. Surely the son is mindful of his own sin, but it's as if the father doesn't care about that nonsense right now. I'm not saying God doesn't care about sin; I'm saying that sin, once repented of, isn't on God's mind anymore and He wants to get on with loving us.

The son, on the other hand, has an entirely different narrative playing out in his head: *There is no way Dad is taking me back. I have sinned too much, I have run too far, I have blown too much of the family fortune. My dad's love has surely leaked away.* So he readies his plan to get back into the house. He will tell his dad that he is willing to be a slave, because clearly this is more than he deserves. But his father doesn't let him get the words out of his mouth. He immediately reminds him of his sonship by calling for a ring, a robe, and sandals.

That is the heart of the father.

That is the essence of God.

That is the way He is for me. That is the way He is for you. No strings, no lectures, no expectations ... just love. His son was the very definition of a wretch, but his dad saw through the wreckage, and in his heart, he saw a saint.

In one colossal act of love, the father ripped the faulty sensor out of his son's life.

But do you remember the context? Do you remember *why* Jesus was telling these familiar stories? Don't let the metaphor Jesus painted obscure the objects of the Father's love; those whom God finds very, very valuable are *all sinners.* The prostitutes, the tax collectors, the child abusers, the liars, the cheats, the disobedient, the disrespectful, the idol worshippers, the terrorists, the grandma stealing grapes at the grocery store, the predators, the murderers, the witches, and the human traffickers.

All the sinners.

All of them.

No exceptions.

Not that He doesn't notice their sin or that He winks at it. Sin must be removed and forgiven. But sin is an enemy that God knows well how to deal with.

In each of these stories, a massive search is conducted for a beloved treasure, and the implication is that the search will not end until the treasure is found.

During the summer of 2018, twelve local boys and their soccer coach went missing while exploring a cave system in Thailand. The search parties were willing and determined. Nothing was going to keep them from finding the kids. And when they located the boys and their coach, trapped in nearly impossible circumstances, nothing was going to keep them from rescuing the lost ones. The world was going to see to that. Elon Musk even sent a tiny submarine, which was nice but not helpful.

And just like in each of Jesus's stories, when the boys were rescued, a massive party broke out. One of the most touching parts of the story was the parents who said they weren't going to leave the cave until all the boys were accounted for.

All of them.

And when they were found, they partied.

If your Bible-reading plan has stalled out before you hit Revelation, you may not have seen that a party is how *our* story ends too! It's called the Wedding Feast of the Lamb (Revelation 19), and Jesus is waiting for us, even holding off on drinking until the partying commences (Matthew 26:29). That's going to be quite a party.

OLDER BROTHERS EVERYWHERE

Unlike the first two parables in Luke 15, this one doesn't *end* with the party. The sheep is found, and there is a party. The coin is found, and there is a party. But when the Prodigal Son is found and the party happens, that's not the end of the story. Jesus drives His point deeper.

Remember, the father had two sons.

> Now his older son was in the field; as he came near the house, he heard music and dancing. So he summoned one of the servants, questioning what these things meant. "Your brother is here," he told him, "and your father has slaughtered the fattened calf because he has him back safe and sound."
>
> Then he became angry and didn't want to go in. So his father came out and pleaded with him. But he replied to his father, "Look, I have been slaving many years for you, and I have never disobeyed your orders, yet you never gave me a goat so that I could celebrate with my friends. But when this son of yours came, who has devoured your assets with prostitutes, you slaughtered the fattened calf for him."

"Son," he said to him, "you are always with
me, and everything I have is yours. But we had
to celebrate and rejoice, because this brother of
yours was dead and is alive again; he was lost and
is found." (Luke 15:25–32 CSB)

The older brother was out in the field working his tail off.
He was dutifully protecting the ninety-nine sheep and keeping
his dad's business going while Pops hung out at the gate waiting
for his other son like an idiot. For all intents and purposes, this
older brother was the better businessman; he was the only one
in this story who made any sense at all.

Like a good, logical rule follower, the older brother isn't
standing next to the father, looking for his brother; he is busy
making things happen. You can almost imagine him out in the
field, working away, thinking about his brother: *I'm glad that
jerk is gone. I can't believe Dad hangs out by that gate looking for
him every day. When will he see who his only decent son is?*

Now, we need to remember that this is a parable, not a
true-life account of a real father and sons. But it's fun to specu-
late. I imagine that the older brother was probably ticked when
his brother actually came home. If he *had* been at the gate, I
suspect he would've tried to prevent his father from letting the
fool back in.

Another thing that strikes me about this story is how the
older brother is portrayed. Here's what he says to his dad: "Look
how many years I've stayed here serving you, never giving you

one moment of grief, but have you ever thrown a party for me and my friends?" (Luke 15:29 THE MESSAGE).

Never. One. Moment. Of. Grief.

Liar. Let's be honest—can any son say that?

But do you see the posture of God, represented by the father, to the older brother who thought way too highly of himself? It was the same posture He had for the younger brother.

> "Son," he said to him, "you are always with me, and everything I have is yours. But we had to celebrate and rejoice, because this brother of yours was dead and is alive again; he was lost and is found." (Luke 15:31–32 CSB)

Love.

That is the posture of God toward wretches—both the wretches who run away from home and the ones who stay.

God knows that Satan is screaming lies in our ears. He's not surprised when we believe them and act on them as if they're true. But neither does He believe those lies. When we come back to Him, nothing has changed about how He loves us. He's ready to get on with the business of living together as Father and child.

CHAPTER 6

CHERISHED WHORE

*A PARABLE OF BETRAYAL. MORE BETRAYAL. AND A
LOVE THAT TRANSCENDS IT ALL.*

José sat on the saggy edge of a twin-size cot wondering if (or more likely *when*) he was going to need a new bed. He had always enjoyed the solitude of his one-bedroom apartment, but for the first time it was feeling a bit cramped. Soon, his wife would be moving in. That is, once he convinced someone to marry him. Not just anyone. He was looking for a woman with a … unique … background. After taking one more pensive look around, he grabbed his wallet and keys and headed for the door.

Thirty minutes later, as he parked his car on the wrong kind of street in the wrong part of town, he began to question his own sanity. Had he really heard the voice of God, or was he losing his mind? He had always considered himself a level-headed, pragmatic dude. Maybe he needed to take a minute before doing something so drastic.

No. It *was* God. José was sure of it.

Before he could change his mind, he jumped out of the car, locked the door (and double-checked it as he looked again at his surroundings), and purposefully strode through the entrance of the run-down, shady roadside bar.

As his eyes adjusted to the darkness and the smoke, his mind adjusted to the task at hand and he thought, *How do I even do this?*

Perched atop a creaky barstool, José ordered a drink, then scanned the room for activity he wanted no part of. Before he could even take a sip, the first in what would become a long line of women touched his shoulder. As each hooker sought to gain access to his affections (and his wallet), he felt his heart sink.

This was not what he had signed up for. Come to think of it, he hadn't *signed up* for anything! This wasn't even his idea. As he took one last gulp from the bottom of his dirty glass, he made up his mind.

He was going home.

He threw a few bills on the counter and began to rise from his stool just as *she* sat on his lap. "No, thanks," he muttered at the exact same moment as she said, "I'm Destiny; what's your name?"

As he peered into her eyes, all he could think was *Destiny? What a cliché.* But maybe this exquisite woman would live up to her name. He wanted to say, "What is a beautiful woman like you doing in a place like this?" but he clamped his teeth down on his tongue before he ruined his chances with a tired old line he was sure she had heard countless times before.

Realizing she was still on his lap, José gently moved her onto the stool next to him. "Is *Destiny* your real name?"

She laughed flirtatiously. "Of course."

Over the next hour, two things became apparent, one to her and one to him. To her, it was apparent that this guy wasn't like the rest of the men who came to this particular bar at this particular time of day. To him, it was apparent that he was going to marry a stunning woman who didn't yet know she was *his* destiny.

The thought of committing to this woman terrified José. Who was she? Why was she here, doing this? Did she want to be here? Would she want to come with him?

No "transaction" occurred that night, nor any of the nights that followed. But the creaky stool at the end of the bar became José's nightly perch. Sometimes Destiny was there, and sometimes she wasn't. When she was there, they would talk. How nice their talks were. More times than José was comfortable with, she would have to leave to "work." But she always came back to sit down next to this unusual man who always listened and never judged. As the weeks went by, her eyes, which had been dulled from years of pain and abuse, began to shine again.

Eventually, she offered José two gifts: her real name—Aiysha—and her company for the entire night *for free*. She was floored by his counter-offer, which was a ring, a husband, a home, and a new life.

José was deliriously happy when he brought Aiysha home to his one-bedroom apartment (*their* one-bedroom apartment now), which he had spent his days sprucing up. It wasn't much, but their love made up for the lack of amenities.

Just when they had figured out a way to make the space work for two, they learned that they were soon to be three. Aiysha was expecting, and José couldn't have been prouder. Each day, as José went off to work, Aiysha hunted for a house they could call a home for their growing family.

One day, she practically leaped through the front door, declaring, "I found it! Let's go, let's go." The house was perfect and they moved in just in time for their son to be born.

That was when reality intruded back into José's life. The voice he'd heard so many months ago, telling him to go out and find a hooker to marry, had been silent so long he'd all but forgotten how this journey had started. Now the voice came back.

"Name your son Trailer Trash."

José's stomach turned. *Trailer Trash?* What would people in the cul-de-sac think?

This command would have seemed categorically unthinkable if it hadn't come from the same voice that had told him,

"Marry a whore." So he did it. Aiysha wasn't pleased, but he prevailed.

Despite the voice's bizarre commands and his new son's name, José was deliriously happy, and the talk around town about his son's name did nothing to dampen his spirits. Before Trailer Trash could even walk, bun number two was in the oven, and José's heart rose through the roof.

As expected, the baby-name book in the sky spoke audibly and gave the name for José's beautiful baby daughter: "Name her Unloved." As if a son named Trailer Trash wasn't enough, he now had a cute little baby girl named Unloved. José began to wonder if this voice represented the words of something more sinister than God. There was no way God had a sick sense of humor, was there?

As José and Aiysha walked their children around town, it began to bug him how often people commented on how much the kids looked like their mom but never about how they resembled him. Not once. As Unloved grew, so did the accusations.

It finally dawned on José that maybe Aiysha, his beautiful wife, had not left her old life behind. What lies had she believed about him or herself that had made her think she should go back to it?

José wanted answers, and he got them as he stood in the delivery room waiting for his third child to be born. Whether it was the pain of childbirth or the drugs that were supposed to keep it at bay, he would never know, but as his second son was born, Aiysha's mouth was loosened and José learned he wasn't the father. In fact, she couldn't be sure that any of the children really belonged to him.

Crushed, José stumbled into the street, gasping for fresh air and some sort of explanation from God. "How could You? This is exactly what I was afraid of!" His anger turned to despair. "I should never have listened to You."

Just then, the first cry of the newborn baby mixed with the cry of a broken man.

And the voice of almighty God spoke again. "Call him Bastard."

"Are you kidding me?"

"Bastard."

"That's all You can say to me?"

José turned and pushed his way back into the delivery room and spoke four words that stung everyone in the room: "His name is Bastard." Then he turned to his wife. "Pack your things."

Destiny left behind her home, her children, and the only man who had ever loved her and called her Aiysha, and she went back to the life she had never really left behind.

José stayed in a house that felt simultaneously empty and full. It was empty of the love of his wife and yet full of three little reminders that she was gone. He became a single father raising two children that weren't even his own—Unloved and Bastard.

Yet how could he put his anger on these innocent children? To him, they were his own. José loved these children with the kind of pure love that he'd once had for Aiysha—a love he'd thought had died forever.

José and the kids learned to go it alone. As toddlers turned to teens and diapers were swapped for diplomas, the ache of Aiysha's absence faded into a dull memory.

When Bastard, the youngest, moved out, José couldn't bear the sight of the empty house anymore, so he sold it. He moved back into a cramped one-bedroom apartment that looked eerily similar to the one he'd lived in when he'd first heard the voice so long ago.

That first night in the apartment, José did what he did every day: he knelt by the side of the bed and prayed for the strength to take one more breath.

The voice came back. "Go get her."

God didn't have to say who. Who else could it have been? But José wanted to know why and how!

"You want me to do *what*? But she's gone. Can't You see? She's not coming back. Besides, I don't even know if I want her back. How am I supposed to love her again? And how would I even know where to look for her?"

Of course, he already knew.

Fifteen minutes later, he pulled his car onto a dimly lit street that hadn't changed in twenty years. The bar looked unchanged too. *I can't believe that place is still here.* He got out of the car and headed toward the door.

He had taken only five steps when he saw, right there in the filth of the alley, the battered and discarded body of his sweet Aiysha. She was half-naked, arms dotted with needle marks, and beaten, probably by her so-called lovers. Instantly, the walls of

José's heart crumbled, and he collapsed next to her body. He caressed her forehead and found himself amazed that he still loved her. He tenderly worked his arms under her back and legs and picked her up.

"What are you doing?" growled the hulking shadow of a man.

"I'm taking her home."

"Not without paying first!"

José rested Aiysha on the ground and emptied his pockets onto the wet pavement. He didn't wait to see if the man would be satisfied. He scooped up Aiysha again and put her into his car.

Back in his one-bedroom apartment (*their* one-bedroom apartment), he cleaned her wounds on his saggy cot and held her close. He tended to her with gentleness even as the drugs left her system and her body demanded their return.

She opened her eyes and recognized José. He swept a lock of hair from her face. No words were spoken at first, but it was understood: she was his again, and he was hers.

Each day as she recovered, he held her face in his hands and gently but firmly spoke the future into her soul: "No more lovers, Aiysha. Only love. Only me."

IT'S NOT ACTUALLY A PARABLE BECAUSE IT'S BASED ON A TRUE STORY

True confession time: My skill as a writer is not nearly high enough that I could come up with that story. It's an embellishment of an account I straight-up plagiarized from the Bible. Actually, I took quite a few liberties with the biblical story to modernize it while trying to keep the punch in the gut from the original. The truth that is so gripping in the biblical account is that, even when God's "beloved" betrays Him, He receives them (or her) back and provides redemption.

It's a story about love, betrayal, and love restored. It's a love story about a man named Hosea (not José) and a woman named Gomer (not Aiysha … although both names mean the same thing: "complete"). It's the true love story of God and His love for Israel.

And it's the story of God loving you and me. He knows that, every day in little and big ways, we abandon Him and run after other lovers—the sin we seem to love more than Him. The stories we believe about ourselves that keep us in our old ways. That's what the book of Hosea is driving at.

To me, though, the question that leaps from the pages is not why would Hosea take Gomer back, but why would God take *us* back?

Sin is a really big deal.

It is such a big deal that God never minimizes the rebellion and rejection that sin represents, nor does He downplay the effects sin has on our relationship with Him. This is what we see in the book of Hosea. The pain of sin is real. The pain is raw. It is not to be glossed over.

When Hosea realizes what his wife has done, God gives him words that both reflect his pain and echo God's pain:

Plead with your mother, plead—
    for she is not my wife,
    and I am not her husband—
that she put away her whoring from her face,
    and her adultery from between her breasts;
lest I strip her naked
    and make her as in the day she was born,
and make her like a wilderness,
    and make her like a parched land,
    and kill her with thirst. (Hosea 2:2–3)

This isn't just Hosea's description of Gomer; it's God's description of us when we believe lies about ourselves and act accordingly.

Whore.

Too many real-life stories of betrayal end there, triggering a lifetime of bitterness. But that is not the end of the story for Gomer or for us. As Hosea rescues Gomer from her sin, he says to her (and God says to Israel, and Jesus says to us):

Therefore, behold, I will allure her,
    and bring her into the wilderness,
    and speak tenderly to her.
And there I will give her her vineyards
    and make the Valley of Achor a door
        of hope....

> And I will betroth you to me forever. I will
> betroth you to me in righteousness and in justice,
> in steadfast love and in mercy. I will betroth you
> to me in faithfulness. And you shall know the
> LORD. (Hosea 2:14–15, 19–20)

How amazing that God starts with a "therefore." That word is used when the reasons, when the "becauses," have been laid out and it's time to outline the consequences. Because of the bad news. Because we are such sinners. Because we cannot save ourselves. Because all that we can be accused of (and more) is true. Because we are whores. Because of the unfathomable betrayal.

Because of all that, therefore … what? What will God do as a consequence to all those sins?

"Behold, I will allure her."

In the wilderness of the pain we have brought on ourselves, God speaks to us tenderly. And when He does, the wilderness becomes a vineyard and the vineyard a door of hope.

In my version of Hosea's story, Gomer's (Aiysha's) sin wore her out. It has that effect on me too. Then, when the world had beaten her up and left her for dead, Hosea paid everything to buy her back.

Can you feel the enormity of what he did? Have you ever seen a better picture of God's grace? Not only for Gomer or for Israel, but for any human who has ever lived or ever will live. Isn't this a portrait of us—and not only before we come to Christ in salvation, but even after salvation? He brings us in and gives us a new, amazing life, and after a while we go back to our whoring. Back to our sins. Back to the squalid life we had before.

This once-beautiful woman was now beaten and ashamed and strung out and in the worst shape of her life, and yet Hosea bought her back. He looked past what the world saw in her and what the lies in her head told her about herself, and he perceived beauty that only true love could see.

God's redemption didn't stop with Gomer. In José's story, their children were named Trailer Trash, Unloved, and Bastard. In the book of Hosea, God had him name his children Jezreel (God Scatters), Lo-Ruhamah (Not Loved, or No Mercy), and Lo-Ammi (Not Mine, or Not My People).

Then He changed their names ... and their destinies:

> And in that day I will answer, declares the LORD,
>> I will answer the heavens,
>> and they shall answer the earth,
> and the earth shall answer the grain, the wine,
>>> and the oil,
>> and they shall answer Jezreel,
>> and I will sow her for myself in the land.
> And I will have mercy on No Mercy,
>> and I will say to Not My People, "You are
>>> my people";
>> and he shall say, "You are my God."
>> (Hosea 2:21–23)

The gospel plot of Hosea and Gomer has a glorious gospel subplot.

(Another translation of the Hebrew behind the word "answer" in the passage above is "hear" or "pay attention to." *So Jezreel was no longer scattered or driven away but was hearkened to and preferred. No Mercy [or Unloved] would receive mercy and love. And Not My People would be adopted and embraced and become His People.*)

The people most hurt by Gomer's sin were washed clean alongside her. The curses that came because of sin—even punishment on innocent children—were wholly reversed, and the children's standing before God was established and redeemed.

As God transforms sinners to saints, His love ripples out into the lives of the sinners all around those He is saving. One by one, the lies His children believe fall away, and this overflows to people around them.

You can see this even in one of the most hated men in America.

Larry Nassar.

His name brings bile to many throats and rage to many hearts.

In recent memory, no one is more undeserving of grace than this monster. He is a convicted child molester with hundreds of innocent young victims, many of them involved with the US gymnastics program.

His horrific story played out on international media and in my backyard. Although I never met the man, at one time he lived a couple of blocks from my house. A number of his victims attend or attended my church. The setting for his crimes was my beloved Michigan State University and my home city of Lansing.

When the time came for Nassar's sentencing, our entire community was buzzing about Judge Rosemarie Aquilina's decision to allow all of his victims the opportunity to make victim-impact statements. One hundred fifty-six of them took her up on the offer.

One hundred fifty-six.

As I sat in my office watching the statements, one stood out above the others: the statement of Rachael Denhollander, the first woman to publicly accuse Nassar of abuse. After a stunning indictment of his crimes and the lasting effects on her life, she took a deep breath and preached one of the best sermons on grace I have ever heard.

> In our early hearings, you brought your Bible into the courtroom and you have spoken of praying for forgiveness. And so it is on that basis that I appeal to you. If you have read the Bible you carry, you know the definition of sacrificial love portrayed is of God himself loving so sacrificially that he gave up everything to pay a penalty for the sin he did not commit. By his grace, I, too, choose to love this way.
>
> You spoke of praying for forgiveness. But, Larry, if you have read the Bible you carry,

you know forgiveness does not come from doing good things, as if good deeds can erase what you have done. It comes from repentance which requires facing and acknowledging the truth about what you have done in all of its utter depravity and horror without mitigation, without excuse, without acting as if good deeds can erase what you have seen in this courtroom today.

The Bible you carry says it is better for a millstone to be thrown around your neck and you thrown into a lake than for you to make even one child stumble. And you have damaged hundreds.

The Bible you speak carries a final judgment where all of God's wrath and eternal terror is poured out on men like you. Should you ever reach the point of truly facing what you have done, the guilt will be crushing. And that is what makes the gospel of Christ so sweet. Because it extends grace and hope and mercy where none should be found. And it will be there for you.

I pray you experience the soul crushing weight of guilt so that you may someday experience true repentance and true forgiveness from God, which you need far more than forgiveness from me—though I extend that to you as well.[1]

Larry Nassar's vile crimes seem unforgivable—but they are not, because "the gospel of Christ [is] so sweet. Because it extends grace and hope and mercy where none should be found. And it will be there for [him]."

Do you see the implication? Rachael is saying she is hoping to spend eternity with Larry Nassar, the man who coldly and calculatingly abused her and hundreds of others. Does that blow your mind the way it blows mine? Wow.

Only grace can do that. Only the realization that a person doesn't do things like he did unless he's come to believe powerful lies about himself, others, and God.

CHAPTER 7

LOVING THE UNLOVABLE

THERE'S NO SUCH THING AS A LITTLE BIT OF GRACE

Way too early one morning, I was being tortured at the hands of a dental hygienist. As she picked away at my gum line, we (well, mostly *she*) talked about our kids. Midway through a particularly excruciating scrape, she declared, "Of course, you were probably a good kid."

Good thing my mouth was full of dental instruments and agony so I couldn't protest. *You have no idea.*

I often refer to myself as a "recovering hypocrite." I do it not to be clever or coy, but to be honest. Each and every day, I feel the gravity of sin pulling me toward duplicity. *You have no idea.*

Why would a holy and perfect and pure God love people like Gomer, or Israel, or you and me?

Because God is love.

He's not just a good example of love or the best model of love. He *is* love (1 John 4:8). Even if (or rather, when) we deny His love, He just keeps pressing on.

There's an incredibly sad Korean phrase with no good English equivalent. The phrase is 짝사랑 (*"Jjak Sa Lang"*), and the closest translation we have is "one-way love," but that doesn't do it justice.

The word is woeful because it describes unrequited love. It's a word about loving someone who doesn't love you back.

I don't know about you, but I've seen my fair share of broken trust in relationships—the kind that makes me want to shout *never again*! But any pain you or I have had in this arena is a blip on the radar compared with the shattered relationships God has experienced. You and I (and all of humankind) break His trust over and over and over and over and over, and He loves us, He loves us, He loves us, He loves us, He loves us.

Why do we need to keep being reminded of His love? It doesn't leak away, after all, so that we have to top off the tank continually with reminders that His love is *still* there. We do break His trust and He does keep loving us, but I think we keep needing those reminders only because of a faulty sensor that says the tank is moving toward "empty." When we can identify that warning light as false, we can see that God's love is vacuum sealed inside us and no tool or accident ever created will cause any leak in that system. And then maybe we won't need those reminders.

You see, we think of love as a two-way street. "You gotta meet me halfway, baby!" But what if your partner has a bad day, a bad week, a bad month, or a bad life? In those times, we so quickly throw love away. As soon as one person breaks trust, we think the whole relationship is in the tank. How can we love again? How can we trust again? What if we get hurt again?

But God's not like that.

For God, *Jjak Sa Lang* (one-way love) isn't sad—it's His glorious plan for the universe. Loving the unlovable is who He is: "If we are faithless, he remains faithful—for he cannot deny himself" (2 Timothy 2:13).

How scandalous!

It is at the core of who God is to love the unlovable! He can't help Himself.

It is easy to think that God loves only good people who do good things, but God loves sinners! God loves us even when we betray Him. When we, of our own doing, enslave ourselves to sin and walk away from Him, He buys us back, and at a horrific price. Just ask José.

In fact, it's more accurate to say He initially purchased us with such a hefty sum that we have an infinite credit line to spend on our sin. I don't mean He's given us carte blanche to sin as much as we want.

> What should we say then? Should we continue in sin so that grace may multiply? Absolutely not! How can we who died to sin still live in it? (Romans 6:1–2 CSB)

I mean only that He doesn't have to buy us *back* because no one can rip us from His hand.

> You were ransomed from the futile ways inherited from your forefathers, not with perishable things such as silver or gold, but with the precious blood of Christ, like that of a lamb without blemish or spot. (1 Peter 1:18–19)

The price God paid for you was the life of His Son, Jesus.

We, like Gomer (and Hosea, Larry Nassar, and everyone else who has ever lived, for that matter), deserve humiliation and death because of our sin. We just do. We tend to downplay the severity of our discretions because we have this propensity to sanitize our sins to present ourselves to God as something more than we are.

It's not adultery—it's *an affair*, we prefer to say.

It's not a lie—it's *a half truth*.

Come on! Let's call it like it is. Our adultery, our lying, and all the other sins we commit make us *spiritual harlots* deserving of humiliation and death. In fact, the Bible even refers to sin that we commit unconsciously or unwittingly (Leviticus 4:2–3,

13–14; Luke 12:47–48). Our sin is so deep that sometimes we don't even know we are doing it. Until we recognize and accept the enormity of our sin, we will never hope to fully realize God's grace toward us. Only when the bad news is bad enough can we grasp the good news.

The depth of our sin makes our salvation all the more astonishing. Author Jefferson Bethke reminds us that God's grace doesn't wait for us to clean ourselves up:

> Grace isn't there for some future me but for the real me. The me who struggled. The me who was messy. The me who was addicted to porn. The me who didn't have all the answers. The me who was insecure. He loved me in my mess; he was not waiting until I cleaned myself up.[1]

This is the message of the gospel:

> For while we were still helpless, at the right time, Christ died for the ungodly. For rarely will someone die for a just person—though for a good person perhaps someone might even dare to die. But God proves his own love for us in that while we were still sinners, Christ died for us. How much more then, since we have now been declared righteous by his blood, will we be saved through him from wrath. (Romans 5:6–9 CSB)

And only when we grasp the good news that God has eternally wrapped us in His love can we understand that the voices saying we are out of His love are false. Only then can we realize that sin doesn't satisfy, but neither does it change who we are in God's eyes.

That's the wily nature of sin. We pursue it tentatively. Then, when we have had a taste, we can become enamored and it can take over our lives even as we become more and more disgusted by our own actions. Trapped in our own net, convinced that the warning light on our dashboard is correct in how it defines us, we just can't stop. It's like an addiction.

Josh was riding his bike with some friends when they came across an unusual-looking paper bag on the side of the street. Wondering what kind of treasure they had stumbled upon, he jumped off his bike, ran to the bag, and dumped its contents onto the street. As soon as the magazines began to slide out of the bag, the kids knew they had both hit pay dirt and found something they had to hide. They stuffed the porn magazines back into the bag as fast as they could so that no one driving by would catch the glimpse of skin that had instantly captured the young men's imaginations and budding libidos. They hurried to Josh's house and locked the door to his room to have a look.

As the boys giggled and laughed at the images in the magazine, something began to stir in the back of Josh's mind. That stirring, and the images associated with it, became the start of a lifelong struggle with porn. Over the years, he was simultaneously titillated and disgusted by himself so much that he hid his secret from everyone. That was, until the search history on his phone became the last straw that ended a difficult marriage.

You know what that sin is in your life. Just mentioning the topic probably brings it right to your mind.

Maybe it was a onetime thing. Maybe it's something you can't seem to stop. But the thought of it sits like a stone in the pit of your stomach. Maybe you have pursued power or money or pleasure or the appreciation of others and have ruined your marriage and the relationships with your kids in the process. You can't bear to look at yourself or what you have done. You wish you could just go back in time.

We see that in the repeated descriptions of Israel in the Old Testament. Personified as a woman in Ezekiel 23, she remembered what it was like when she was young, and she fantasized about it and pursued it, hoping to capture some of the glory she felt in those days. The voices in her mind fed her whatever they had to in order to keep her from becoming who she was destined to be. And she didn't have the benefit of the Holy Spirit, as we do. So she plunged into her old, familiar sin. But it didn't satisfy. Her sin was leading to destruction.

It's wretched.

Let's call it like it is. Every sinful attitude, every sinful action, is a betrayal to God. It's no wonder that one of the most common pictures of the effects of sin in the Bible is that of a jilted lover.

And yet …

To terrible sinners, God offers righteousness and justice. To the one deep in disgusting, harmful sin, He offers grace.

Whoa there! Hold on. Oh no! We don't want *bad* sinners receiving grace. *That* person doesn't deserve grace. Not that jerk. Not that fallen Christian leader. Not that predator who used his position to prey on the innocent. Not that woman who used her apparent righteousness to cloak her horrible sin. No. Nope. Not happening. The only part of Jesus's hand of mercy those people deserve is the *back* of it as He slaps them into outer darkness.

Oh yes, we do indeed want them to receive grace. If they aren't eligible for God's grace, then neither are you or me. The justice of God was poured out on Jesus. The punishment for our whoredom was paid by Christ, and we've been washed clean by His blood. The righteousness of Jesus was then transferred forever in steadfast love and mercy to us. To the whores.

Besides, grace says more about the giver than the receiver. Paul Zahl reminds us that grace is the definition of *Jjak Sa Lang*:

> Grace is love that seeks you out when you have nothing to give in return. Grace is love coming at you that has nothing to do with you. Grace is being loved when you are unlovable....
>
> Grace is a love that has nothing to do with you, the beloved. It has everything and only to do with the lover.... It reflects a decision on the part of the giver, the one who loves, in relation to the receiver, the one who is loved, that negates any qualifications the receiver may personally hold.... Grace is *one-way love*.[2]

The one-way love of God means that you were a plain old wretch, but because of His grace, now you are a wretched saint.

What do we do with a God like that?

What do we do with a love like that?

Maybe you have spent your whole life trying not to look at the dark, broken parts of yourself. You stuff them down. The voices shouting in your ear describe you in such horrible terms that the only way you can move forward is to not think about them. You secretly judge or quietly compare yourself to others, and that helps you feel better about yourself. But those (false) messages still haunt you.

Tim Keller once said that cultures often have "unexamined assumptions of superiority."[3] People do too. Sometimes the barrier that keeps us from embracing the grace of God is that we don't examine our assumption of superiority.

"I'm not that bad," we say to ourselves. "At least compared to *that guy*" (see Luke 18:11). Yeah, you are. You are much, much worse. And so am I.

I'm not saying you should hate yourself. This isn't "proof" that you really are outside of God's love. But when we can drop our "I'm okay because at least I…" facade, and once we get that deep in our souls, it sets us free so we don't have to put up a front. We can let our guards down and admit there are deep, dark spots in our lives. Because our sanctification isn't complete yet, and because we still pay attention to faulty sensors.

God, in His love, relentlessly seeks out fallen, broken, and messy people who are willing to admit that about themselves and who are willing to receive His love at face value, with no strings attached. And for those who really receive it, there comes the desire to change. To become more like God and the love that He offers. To stop acting as if malfunctioning sensors are pointing to actual malfunctions. That's what the love of God does. It doesn't require that you become a better person in order to receive it; it simply asks that you receive it, and because of it you become a better person.

Philip Yancey reminds us that:

> Grace means there is nothing we can do to make God love us more—no amount of spiritual calisthenics and renunciations, no amount of knowledge gained from seminaries and divinity schools, no amount of crusading on behalf of righteous causes. And grace means there is nothing we can do to make God love us less—no amount of racism or pride or pornography or adultery or even murder. Grace means that God already loves us as much as an infinite God can possibly love.[4]

So how *do* you respond to that kind of love?

You can ignore it, I suppose. You can go about your life pretending that it doesn't exist and that you don't really need it, even though there's a longing in your soul that you can't fill. However, it's nearly impossible to offer grace to others when you haven't received it yourself. The deeper grace goes, the more you can extend it to others.

When you begin to see yourself as you really are, you become open to change. God's grace sees you as fallen, broken, messy, and in need of a love that accepts you where you are.

When you cry out to God asking for His love to save you, you can get honest with Him about the other lovers you've been running to.

And He will throw open His arms and say, "You are wretched. You are beautiful. *You are loved.*"

CHAPTER 8

YET, HERE WE ARE

PLAYING NICE WITH A TYRANT

Sometimes, when I reflect on the state of the world, I can't help but think, *I could do this better.* I'm not just talking about the local coffee shop and the federal tax code, but the whole world. Especially this whole "making Christians" thing.

If *I* were God, I would snap my fingers like Thanos in the *Avengers* movies, and every man, woman, and child would be saved in a single dramatic scene. Pain and sorrow would disappear—not in some far-off future, but this instant! I mean, why wait? Of course, if God wanted to keep some semblance of free will, He could wait until someone chose to follow Him and *then* He could snap His fingers and make the magic happen.

Come to think of it, that's the way to go: let sin run its course, and when a person can't take it any longer and makes a profession of faith, *POOF,* everything in their life locks into place perfectly. Their relationships become sweeter, illnesses are healed, and daffodils sprout up from their footsteps. Perfection all around.

What a great evangelistic tool that approach to salvation would be! Everyone would want to be a Christian.

The more I think about this, the more I really think God may have messed up here. If only He were as smart as me!

Now, of course, before I get struck by lightning, I should probably mention that my tongue is firmly planted in my cheek. Although, even if I *weren't* kidding, that would be okay with God. Seriously.

Christian philosopher Alvin Plantinga postulates that two things must be true. First, we must be living in a world where God exists. Second, we must be living in the one world, out of an infinite number of possible alternate worlds, in which this God gets the most glory. Plantinga derives this notion not from the Bible (which obviously supports the idea) but from logic.[1]

In an overly simplistic nutshell, here's how Plantinga arrives at his second conclusion (you can read more about his first conclusion by following the link in the endnotes). Assuming for the moment that there *is* an all-powerful God, this being would be able to conceive of every possible world faster than Dr. Strange (sorry about all the Marvel references). He could imagine a world where water buffalo fly, another world in which bacon-wrapped bacon is considered the greatest delicacy (wait, that's *this* world, isn't it?), and yet another world in which I am the ultimate athlete. Every possible world is a world God could have created.

If that's true, then that list includes the world in which He snaps his fingers and instantly removes all pain. The world where Christians don't have to experience hurt once they believe in Him. This means He imagined that world but decided not to create it. Why? He has a reason He didn't create that world—and a pretty good one too.

That world wouldn't have given Him *maximum* glory.

Somehow, beyond our wildest imaginations, only the world we live in gives Him maximum glory. The world in which you and I live as wretched saints. It's not just logical; it's God's plan to give you and me the greatest chance to know Him intimately.

> The God who made the world and everything in it, being Lord of heaven and earth, does not live in temples made by man, nor is he served by human hands, as though he needed anything, since he himself gives to all mankind life and breath and everything. And he made from one man every nation of mankind to live on all the face of the earth, having determined allotted periods and the boundaries of their dwelling place, that they should seek God, and perhaps feel their way

toward him and find him. Yet he is actually not
far from each one of us. (Acts 17:24–27)

In other words, you are exactly where you need to be, where
you *must* be. No other world would do.

That means you can relax, because no matter how it may
appear, things are as they ought to be. Unfortunately, it doesn't
always feel that way. We are told that if we are to be good
Christians, we need to make some fundamental changes to our
behavior.

Here's a passage in the Bible that gets deployed a lot as a
weapon:

> Therefore, brothers and sisters, in view of the
> mercies of God, I urge you to present your bodies
> as a living sacrifice, holy and pleasing to God;
> this is your true worship. Do not be conformed
> to this age, but be transformed by the renewing
> of your mind, so that you may discern what
> is the good, pleasing, and perfect will of God.
> (Romans 12:1–2 CSB)

We're often told that this means we have to get all our sins
fixed and stop being such screw-ups. But let's consider what these
verses are truly saying.

For the first eleven chapters of Romans, the author (the apostle
Paul) lays out both bad news and good news in substantial doses.

He talks about the destructive nature of man's sin, which gets so bad that God washes His hands of His creation. Then, he swings to the extraordinary gift of Jesus's life and death, which saves those who commit these sins. He calls on his reader to repent, and yet he laments his own inability to do so fully (Romans 7). Reading straight through the book can give you mental whiplash. It's almost as if he is saying over and over …

We are wretched.

We can be saints.

I am wretched.

I can be a saint.

You are wretched.

You can be a saint.

We are wretched saints.

You and I are being transformed by the relentless grace of God. That's the context of Romans 12, in fact. Because we are wretched saints, he can start chapter 12 with a "therefore." Let's look again at the passage:

> Therefore, brothers and sisters, in view of the mercies of God, I urge you to present your bodies as a living sacrifice, holy and pleasing to God; this is your true worship. Do not be conformed to this age, but be transformed by the renewing of your mind, so that you may discern what is the good, pleasing, and perfect will of God. (Romans 12:1–2 CSB)

To treat this passage as a weapon—*Why don't you get your life together?*—is to tragically ignore its context. I think what Paul is saying is so much more powerful and profound.

I think he's saying that, yes, as a follower of Jesus you are to present yourself to Him as a sacrifice—but as a very specific type of sacrifice: a living one. You are to live *in view of the mercies of God*. Not perfectly sinless, but in view of God's mercies. In other words, don't live as if you are still under the law or under some sort of pressure to perform. Live as the wretched saint you are; that's God's plan for your life.

Even the command "do not be conformed to this age" is followed by words that might most literally be translated "keep on being transformed by the renewing of your mind." He's saying that your transformation is what God has planned for you.

Let me say it another way: you are *meant* to be a wretched saint. This is so that God, through the power of the Holy Spirit, can transform your wretchedness into the likeness of Jesus, until all that is left is the saint part. When you are tempted to think God isn't pleased with you, remember that you are right where He wants you.

THE SERMON KIM JONG-UN RUINED

And just like that, the sermon I had labored over (but never preached) was outdated.

I can't believe Kim Jong-Un would do that to me. Of course, he probably wasn't thinking about me (as shocking as that sounds), but he had royally messed me up.

The North Korean dictator was tragically unaware that I try to write my sermons a few weeks in advance. This practice is helpful for people on my team who do all the heavy lifting that surrounds my teaching to make it work (discussion questions, presentation graphics, worship songs, and stuff like that). While there are a lot of benefits to getting everything done that far out, there is one definite downside—a downside that the wily Kim had unwittingly exploited.

The big hook for my suddenly defunct sermon was how peace and denuclearization on the Korean peninsula were not in the cards. Ever. Or at least not any time soon.

It was a great sermon, if I do say so myself. That was, until the Thursday in April 2018 before I preached it. On that particular Thursday, I sat stunned with the rest of the world as Kim Jong-Un stepped across the South Korean border to shake hands with Moon Jae-In, the president of South Korea.

Unbelievable.

Later that day, they walked down the street holding hands. *Holding hands!* They kept holding hands through a press conference while their wives stood next to them, receiving none of the affection their husbands were sharing.

The new BFFs even went to a K-pop concert! I have to admit I would've been more than a little bit jealous if I hadn't been so ticked.

Remember, this was Thursday. I was preaching Saturday. The pivotal hook of my sermon—written weeks before—was centered on the Kim regime's stubborn unwillingness to negotiate, even if it meant sacrificing their survival and the flourishing of the North Korean people.

Seriously, how could I have predicted this turn of events?

Once I began to get over myself (which I'm ashamed to say took way longer than it should have), I began to wonder what the South Koreans thought of the whole thing. I wondered how many of them thought, *How dare our president hold hands with that man.* Let's not forget that this is the guy who executed his political enemies with anti-aircraft artillery. His record of human rights abuses is on par with some of the worst tyrants in history.

Political motivations and strategies aside, the picture that unfolded on screens around the world can best be summarized in one word: *grace*. When Moon extended his hand across the border to a brutal dictator, he was extending grace.

Normally, politics are a decidedly ungraceful affair, but the joy on these leaders' faces was shockingly authentic. As a middle-aged, white American, I found it difficult to grasp the enormity of the moment until a Korean friend of mine forwarded a Facebook post by Moses Y. Lee to help me understand what was going on.

> To My Non-Korean Friends:
>
> Imagine an alternate universe where the American Civil War ended in stalemate with a formal truce to temporarily stop the fighting. As a result of the war, the American North and South became their own countries even though they

shared the same language, the same history of independence, and the same Western European heritage. And because they were still technically at war, the two nations militarized their borders, planted mines to prevent people from crossing, and focused on restocking/upgrading their military arsenals. The threat of war always loomed over both nations ...

Husbands and wives, fathers and sons, mothers and daughters, brother and sisters—all separated by war. No cross-border communication and visitations are allowed. The South went on to double down on slavery and classism (amongst rich/poor white folks) while the North went on to prosper through open borders, international trade, and free markets. The South memorialized its war heroes and founders such that to even speak ill of them in any way resulted in jail time, not just for you but three generations of your entire family ...

Eventually, Christianity itself became nationalized and syncretized with Southern lore such that nothing of the historical faith remained ...

After sixty years of cold war, the leaders of both nations finally decide to meet face to face for the very first time in history. There's skepticism, an outright sense of betrayal, by many in the

North—both its citizens and former Southerners who escaped. It hurts to see our president playing nice with a war criminal, ruthless tyrant, and genocidal maniac. Yet, here we are.[2]

That might be the best definition of grace I have ever read: "It hurts to see our president playing nice with a war criminal, ruthless tyrant, and genocidal maniac. Yet, here we are."

True grace is messy. That's why rare moments like these stand out. Have you ever noticed how ungraceful grace can be? It's like, the more graceful you try to make grace, the less it works. The only way you can hold hands with the enemy is by the way of grace, and the resulting touch is repulsively tender.

Yet, here we are.

The Kim Jong-Uns in our lives go by lots of names and hold varying levels of tyranny. Mom may not look like a dictator in her church clothes, but you should see her when I don't clean my room. The idiot driving slow in the fast lane is just asking to be forced off the road into a fiery wreck. The years of abuse and neglect keep me from ever wanting to see my ex again, but every week he has to bring the kids over.

And Brian … Don't get me started on Brian.

The pairs of people in these examples live across from each other, separated by a demilitarized zone booby trapped with painful memories, irritating habits, and miles and miles of sin. The sheer notion of extending a hand across that divide is unthinkable!

But that's the crazy thing—it's not grace if the person deserves it.

What if the unthinkable is actually … *thinkable*? What if grace can make the leap across the DMZ in our life? What if Mom and I can start to get along? What if I can smile at the guy driving slow in the fast lane (and mean it)? What if I can positively interact with my ex?

What if I can get along with Brian?

That's going to take a lot of grace.

The Saturday after Kim Jong-Un ruined my sermon, I still had to preach. As the weekend grew closer, I kept waiting for things to take a turn for the worse in the Koreas. That would certainly make my point about the unlikelihood of reconciliation with the dictator even more powerful! Much to my chagrin, peace between these enemies kept looking possible. At the last minute, I hastily rewrote my sermon and preached the original sermon with a half-baked new illustration that, to be honest, I don't even remember. I'm sure no one else does either.

If only I had been preaching on grace. Maybe I would have been able to introduce the congregation to the messy love of God for tyrants like Kim … and me.

DARE TO DEFINE

One problem with grace is that it is shockingly difficult to define. Philip Yancey, who literally wrote the book on grace,[3] won't even attempt it. Asked to give it a go in an interview, he replied simply, "I don't even try."[4]

With all due respect, I think we have to try.

If everything is awesome, nothing is. If everything is abuse, nothing is. If everything is grace, nothing is. We'd better be clear on what we are talking about.

One definition positions grace as the second half of a one-two punch that begins with mercy. Mercy keeps you from getting the negative stuff you *deserve*, and grace swoops in and gives you the positive stuff you *don't deserve*.

Most of the best definitions of grace out there are short enough to fit on a bumper sticker or magnet on your grandma's fridge:

- "Grace is free sovereign favor to the ill-deserving" (B. B. Warfield).[5]
- "Grace is love that cares and stoops and rescues" (John Stott).[6]
- "[Grace] is God reaching downward to people who are in rebellion against Him" (Jerry Bridges).[7]
- "Grace is unconditional love toward a person who does not deserve it" (Paul Zahl).[8]
- "Grace is the good pleasure of God that inclines Him to bestow benefits upon the undeserving" (A. W. Tozer).[9]
- "Grace means undeserved kindness" (Dwight L. Moody).[10]

- "Grace is the goodness of God shown to people who don't deserve it" (John Piper).[11]

All of these definitions are wonderful, beautiful, truthful … and incomplete. Grace is just too difficult to stuff into a neat, little theological box. It's a disruptive pest that gets all up in your business and changes you for the better even when you ignore its effects. The universe runs on grace—but we run *from* it. It's mind-bogglingly simple and irreducibly complex.

Maybe that's why Yancey thought it was so foolish to attempt to define it.

I guess that means I'm a fool, because I'm going to try. Plus, I'm going to up my foolishness by making my definition long and complex. Here goes nothing:

Grace is the ridiculously unwarranted and outrageously favorable posture of God that transforms wretched sinners into wretched saints and keeps at it until they look like Jesus.

We have really been circling around this definition up until this point, but perhaps now would be a good time to think through why defining grace is central to our spiritual growth and why false sensors too often tell us we are failing at it.

Grace is ridiculously unwarranted. You don't deserve it. You will never deserve it. You are a wretch and God doesn't *need* to save you. Your sins against Him are more destructive than you will ever be able to wrap your mind around (Psalm 51:5; Ecclesiastes 7:20; Isaiah 53:6; Luke 7:37–39; Acts 15:11; Romans 5:20; Romans 6:6; Romans 7:14; Romans 8:3; Ephesians 2:1; Titus 2:11; 1 John 1:8).

Grace is outrageously favorable. The love that God extends to wretches like you and me is immeasurable. We gain a complete pardon from our sin, a glorious inheritance as God's adopted children, our brother Jesus's righteousness transferred to our account, and eternal life … just to mention a *smidge* of what God gives us (Psalm 103:12; Micah 7:19; John 1:16; Romans 8:1–2; Colossians 1:12–13; Colossians 3:24; 1 Peter 1:4; 1 Peter 2:9; 1 John 5:11–12).

Grace is the posture of God. Like an athlete who sets his feet in such a way that he is ready to leap in any direction in a split second, God's "feet" are set to launch grace in our direction each and every time we sin (John 1:14; 2 Corinthians 9:8; Hebrews 4:16; Ephesians 1:13; James 4:6).

Grace transforms wretched sinners into wretched saints. We don't become saints by virtue of our own hard work or spiritual discipline, but only by the grace of God through faith (Romans 3:20; Romans 6:14; Romans 11:6; 1 Corinthians 15:9–10; 2 Corinthians 12:8–9; Ephesians 2:8–9; Titus 3:5; Hebrews 13:9; 1 John 1:9).

Grace will keep transforming us until we look like Jesus. The end goal of our sanctification is that we *will* look like Jesus. It's a done deal. It's your destiny. There is no other option on the table. You *will* look like Jesus when God is done with you. The righteousness you already have in God's eyes will be your new eternal reality. The "wretched" will pass away until all that is left is "saint" (Romans 5:21; Romans 8:29; Galatians 2:20; Ephesians 2:10; Colossians 3:4; 2 Corinthians 5:21).

Believing in this magnanimous grace of God is the key to dealing with the faulty sensors that accuse us. When the sensor says, *Wretch*, grace says, *Wretched saint!* When the sensor says, *Run from the scary God*, grace says, *His posture toward you is love.* When the sensor says, *You haven't matured enough in your faith*, grace says, *I'm working on you.* When the sensor says, *You should look more like Jesus*, grace says, *You do and you will.*

For the rest of the book, we will explore how this relentless grace of God transforms the lives not only of wretched saints, but also of everyone around them.

CHAPTER 9

GRACE-RICH GOSPEL THERAPY

INJECTING THE GOOEY GRACE OF GOD INTO YOUR DEEPEST PAIN

My oldest son is a college baseball player. He stepped onto campus his freshman year with a sore elbow from overuse in high school. Before he was allowed to throw a single pitch at the collegiate level, the coaches sent him in for an experimental treatment called platelet-rich plasma (PRP) therapy. The theory is that the plasma in your blood contains healing properties in the form of platelets that can speed up recovery when concentrated enough. The tricky part is getting these platelets to the sore spot, because plasma naturally wants to just wander around your veins all willy-nilly.

That's where PRP comes in. The procedure consists of drawing your own blood, running it through a centrifuge until all the plasma is congealed on top, and then injecting the gooey yellow mixture back into your body at the spot of the soreness.

Eager to get his throwing arm back into shape, my son readily agreed to the treatment. And immediately, he felt worse.

The doctor wiggled the needle around in his tendons (which were already sore), directing the plasma to where he was the weakest. My son later said the injection was the worst pain he had ever felt. Days of pain were followed by weeks when he could barely lift his sore arm. Supposedly this is normal, but that didn't take the pain away.

Slowly, though, pain was replaced with strength. The range of motion in his arm came back. He was able to put pressure on his elbow and flex it in ways he hadn't been able to for a long time. The platelet-rich plasma therapy worked for my son.

Maybe we need *grace-rich gospel therapy.*

As followers of Jesus, we have the gospel flowing through our veins. This gospel is unlike any human experience or interaction we have ever had. It is rich with the healing properties of grace we so desperately need for our interactions with God, others, and ourselves.

Perhaps, in moments of relational and spiritual pain, we need to centrifuge the gooey mess of grace and inject it into our deepest hurts and pettiest annoyances. But I have to warn you: It's going to hurt before it gets better. Because, for this thing to work, we need to inject grace where we hurt the most.

Broken relationships, habitual sin, deep-seated rejection of God, and uncomfortable sin we'd rather not confront—all the things that have resulted from believing faulty sensors—must be the targets of grace.

But take heart. As God's grace goes to work on those areas of weakness, we will become stronger and gain the ability to offer grace to others. We may even be able to extend it to those who caused our pain in the first place. You see, the more we *experience* grace, and the more it is injected into the crustiest parts of our souls, the more it alters our posture toward those who most desperately need it.

That was always the plan.

> Blessed be the God and Father of our Lord Jesus Christ, the Father of mercies and the God of all comfort. He comforts us in all our affliction, so that we may be able to comfort those who are in any kind of affliction, through the comfort we ourselves receive from God. (2 Corinthians 1:3–4 CSB)

The comfort (and grace) that comes to us is given so that we'll pass it along to others.

God doesn't promise to take away our afflictions this side of eternity, but He does promise to comfort us *in* them. It works something like this:

Oh, and by the way, it's likely that you and I receive comfort through another person, right? That means you can add "and from others" under "from God" in the diagram above.

YOUR DEEPEST PAIN IS PART OF GOD'S PLAN FOR OTHERS

Every once in a while, Jesus throws down a statement the whole world remembers. At the top of the list is this one:

> Judge not, that you be not judged. For with the judgment you pronounce you will be judged, and with the measure you use it will be measured to you. Why do you see the speck that is in your

brother's eye, but do not notice the log that is in your own eye? Or how can you say to your brother, "Let me take the speck out of your eye," when there is the log in your own eye? You hypocrite, first take the log out of your own eye, and then you will see clearly to take the speck out of your brother's eye. (Matthew 7:1–5)

We sure do love the "judge not, that you be not judged" part. In fact, we love it so much that we quote it from the King James Version, "Judge not, *lest ye* be judged," because it just has a more sanctimonious air to it.

But there is a remarkable turnabout in this verse. Let's walk through Jesus's logic.

He starts out assuming we have judged someone. And why have we judged? Because someone has done something that deserves judgment, of course! They lied, they cheated, they bullied—most likely, they've done these things to *us*. So we reach into our toolbox of judgments and go after them. Sometimes we pull out an in-your-face *How dare you?* sort of judgment; and sometimes we use the quiet, internal smugness that judges but never verbalizes a single word.

Jesus's response is quite simple, really: "Is that how you would like to be treated?"

Do you want to be cursed at? Would you like the silent treatment? Measure it up, baby, because what you give is what you are going to get.

There's a little quirk of human nature that comes to play in difficult situations like this: *We tend to judge other people the harshest in the areas where we are the weakest.* Whether it is relational conflict, sins we are trapped in, sins that are being committed against us, or a whole host of other murky situations, we are the most severe judges when we ourselves are hurt or guilty.

The fact that your blood boils when your neighbor mows a small patch of your backyard says more about you than him. What do you think he is doing? Claiming it for his own? Our disproportionate reaction to the situation at hand often betrays some sort of woundedness we have not allowed the gospel to penetrate.

My guess is that very few people who know me would describe me as insecure. By all outward appearances, I have a great life and I have been very successful. I am a pastor at a large and growing church. I help start churches all across the midwestern United States and have had the opportunity to preach around the world. I'm an author and I influence thousands of people with my teaching and coaching in person and online. I have an amazing wife, and people often tell me that they hope their kids turn out like ours have. What I lack in athletic ability, I make up for in beard-growing prowess.

And I am *really* insecure.

When I am around other pastors, I feel like a poser because I am a college dropout who never went to seminary (unless you count the unaccredited classes I took a few years back). I still live in the same small part of the country I grew up in, and I have the baked-in sense of inferiority that comes with it.

While I have a fairly good memory for certain meaningless facts and trivia, I often forget where a passage is in the Bible or whether I have met somebody before. In the office and after church services, I frequently panic when someone begins to update me on something they have already told me about and I can't remember a single detail.

I always wonder if the people around me are eventually going to say enough is enough. Maybe that's why the phone call hit me so hard. "We need to talk to you about some stuff," one of my copastors said. "Can you meet for lunch today?"

Oh no.

At lunch that day and over the next few months, I met with several men I respected as they shared with me some of the ways I had interacted with them without enough grace and humility. As they gently reproved me, it became abundantly clear that I had not allowed the grace of God to penetrate my own deep insecurity, and so, when I felt threatened, I would respond from a faulty sensor that was blaring, *You are not enough.* Instead of believing the gospel truth, I even went so far as to label others as insecure in defense of my own behavior.

One of the assignments my copastors gave me was to read the business book *Crucial Conversations*. In this book, the authors noted that when we don't feel safe, we resort to "silence or violence" as a defense (and offense) mechanism.[1] We see this all over the Bible, from the silence of Adam (when he didn't rebuke Eve for eating the forbidden fruit) to the violence of King David (who had Uriah put to death so he could have Uriah's wife).

So take a good hard look: When it comes to judging others, does your violence or your silence betray some insecurity over your own patterns of sin?

Something remarkable happens when you gain this sort of self-awareness and you allow grace to seep into the inkiest places in your soul: You begin to see clearly. Enhanced by an extra hit of grace, you gain perspective, and that allows you to use your newly clear vision to help instead of to judge. There is a world of difference when you are seeing clearly.

This is what my copastors did for me. They took the grace of God and they lovingly injected it into the spot in my soul that needed it the most. Man, did it hurt as they wiggled the needle around and poked and prodded at my pain. But the result is that I feel empowered. In an area of my life I have neglected, I am beginning to feel more and more strength. I sit in meetings now and I can believe what is true—*in Jesus, I am right where I am supposed to be.*

I'm hoping you're beginning to see a superb and uncomfortable implication of all this: Our journey toward experiencing the liberating power of the gospel and extending it to others leads straight through the minefield of our own massive need for grace. Our ability to transfer grace to others is commiserate with the level to which we've been transformed by grace.

WORKERS IN THE VINEYARD

Because Jesus has dealt with sin in such a spectacular fashion, He expects us to follow Him in His pattern of disruptive grace (1 Peter 2:21). As Tim Keller has written, "The more you see your own flaws and sins, the more precious, electrifying, and amazing God's grace appears to you."[2] The natural outcome of experiencing radical forgiveness and grace should be to become more forgiving and gracious.

But why isn't it? I don't know about you, but sometimes I feel I'm trending in the other direction. Why is that?

Let's look at one of Jesus's lesser-talked-about parables.

> For the kingdom of heaven is like a landowner who went out early in the morning to hire workers for his vineyard. After agreeing with the workers on one denarius, he sent them into his vineyard for the day. When he went out about nine in the morning, he saw others standing in the market-place doing nothing. He said to them, "You also go into my vineyard, and I'll give you whatever is right." So off they went. About noon and about three, he went out again and did the same thing. Then about five he went and found others standing around and said to them, "Why have you been standing here all day doing nothing?"

"Because no one hired us," they said to him.

"You also go into my vineyard," he told them. When evening came, the owner of the vineyard told his foreman, "Call the workers and give them their pay, starting with the last and ending with the first."

When those who were hired about five came, they each received one denarius. So when the first ones came, they assumed they would get more, but they also received a denarius each. When they received it, they began to complain to the landowner: "These last men put in one hour, and you made them equal to us who bore the burden of the day's work and the burning heat."

He replied to one of them, "Friend, I'm doing you no wrong. Didn't you agree with me on a denarius? Take what's yours and go. *I want to give this last man the same as I gave you.* Don't I have the right to do what I want with what is mine? Are you jealous because I'm generous?"

So the last will be first, and the first last. (Matthew 20:1–16 CSB)

The landowner is indignant! "Are you seriously upset that I am being generous? Isn't my stuff *my stuff?*"

And look at the landowner's statement embedded in the middle of all of his questions: "I want to give this last man the same as I gave you" (verse 14). That, my friend, is the heart of God. But it is also the part of the gospel that secretly repulses us. Because we see ourselves as uniquely valuable, we want the grace of God poured out on our lives, but we don't really want anyone else to have it.

Think about the person who has hurt you the most. Maybe they are gleefully unaware of the pain you carry deep in your chest. Or maybe they know but just don't care.

Now, in your heart of hearts, do you want God to pour out unfettered love and gobs of grace on *that* person? Come on, be honest. Do you really want God to throw up His arms and declare, "I love you!" to that person? Or do you secretly hope they get what they deserve … while you get *out* of what you deserve?

I had the wonderful gift of men who loved me enough to "gospel my pain." They could have decided I wasn't worth the hassle and discarded me like I've seen happen to so many pastors in similar circumstances. But motivated by the grace of God they had experienced in their own lives, they offered me the same.

At the risk of taking too much creative license with Jesus's story, I wonder what happened next. Did the workers grasp the magnificence of the landowner's generosity; or did they grab their paychecks, storm away, and talk badly about him behind his back?

What about the guys who were hired last? Did receiving full payment for only a fraction of a day's work change them as radically as the woman who was changed when Jesus said of her, "Therefore I tell you, her many sins have been forgiven; that's why she loved much. But the one who is forgiven little, loves little" (Luke 7:47 CSB)?

As I am writing these words, I am sitting in a local coffee shop watching an extremely frustrated man in expensive workout clothes. He got his high-calorie drink (ironic, considering his attire) at the end of the counter, and he immediately looked at it funny. He opened the lid and smelled his drink with a puzzled look on his face. He took a sip and scowled. Then he put the lid back on and headed for the door. Just short of the exit, he stopped and turned around and stood there for a few seconds, deep in thought. In an instant, his whole demeanor changed. Clearly, there was something wrong with his coffee and *it would not do.*

He then began pacing back and forth in front of the pastry counter with a "the sky is falling" look on his face, passive-aggressively trying to get a barista's attention so he could explain how this coffee mix-up had devastated his ability to enjoy his day.

That guy is us, isn't he? We can't even give grace to our coffee. Or our barista.

INVITATION FOR GRACE

Something profound happens when we view the world around us through the lens of the gospel—we begin to see other people's weakness as an invitation for grace.

- We have been forgiven, so we forgive (Ephesians 4:32).

- God has put up with us, so we put up with others (Colossians 3:13).
- We love because God first loved us (1 John 4:19).

Pastor Larry Osborne says that most people won't darken the door of a church unless they have a "need to know" or a "need to grow" moment. Why do people join a Bible study or a small group? They need something. Why do they join a gym? Because they need something.

What if we began to look for "need for grace" moments in others? It's going to necessarily mean messing up our schedules and relationships and pushing us out of our comfort zones. But what if that little bit of commotion is a big part of what God is doing in our life and the life of that other person?

That's the funny thing about grace: It's a disruptive little bugger. It contains a unique power that destroys our finely tuned plans and carefully constructed facades. It exposes the faulty sensors we've believed and leads us back to eternal truth.

Oddly, though, God leaves it up to us how we may choose to respond to that power. The grace of God is so magnanimous that it even allows us to trample it underfoot, and yet it keeps coming at us anyway.

CHAPTER 10

BORN-AGAIN NICK

A CASE STUDY IN GRACE

Certain phrases and stories in the Bible have become so familiar to us that they risk losing their gospel punch. Such is the case with a familiar statement Jesus used with a man He met at the beginning of His public ministry who also had a subtly important role at the end. We'll get to this well-known statement in a minute.

This man, Nicodemus (we'll call him Nick), possessed what anyone would consider the perfect spiritual dashboard. He had an impeccable religious pedigree and a respected position in society. And yet a warning light was blinking. Nick thought it involved Jesus, but it had more to do with a faulty sensor he didn't know he had.

Jesus launched His ministry by going to a party with His friends and turning water into wine when the bar ran dry and the festivities were losing momentum. Soon after, He followed that up with a series of miracles that began to attract a lot of attention. All of this caught the eye of the religious elite, and eventually one of them decided it was time to have a conversation with Him face to face. You've already guessed who it was: Nick.

> Now there was a man of the Pharisees named Nicodemus, a ruler of the Jews. This man came to Jesus by night and said to him, "Rabbi, we know that you are a teacher come from God, for no one can do these signs that you do unless God is with him." (John 3:1–2)

John's description of Nick cues us in on several things about the guy. First, he was intelligent, highly educated, and a respected religious figure. He had everything put together. Also, because he is described as "a ruler of the Jews," we know that he was part of the Sanhedrin, which was the Jewish version of the Supreme Court. Additionally, later in the story, Jesus refers to him as "the teacher of Israel" (John 3:10). Note that he's *the* teacher of Israel, not *a* teacher of Israel. This implies that he was well known in Jerusalem for his teaching ability. Nick knew his Bible very well. He was who you went to if you had any questions.

Ol' Nick was a pretty big deal, in other words.

Somehow he—and presumably other Jewish religious leaders—had heard about the miracles Jesus had been performing, and either on his own accord or in some sort of official capacity, Nick had been sent to scout out Jesus a bit.

If someone were truly performing miracles, as Jesus was, it would constitute a significant situation for all Jews. Throughout the Bible, signs and wonders had preceded the proclamation of some new prophecy. It had been over four hundred years since a prophet had walked in Israel, and so, when Jesus's miracles were reported to them, they knew they needed to check them out.

There's a lot of speculation among scholars as to why Nick came at night. I suspect it was because he wanted a private audience with Jesus where he could be direct with Him. Furthermore, if Jesus turned out to be a crazy person, no one could get on Nick's case for hanging out with Him, since no one would know the two had spoken. It was a win-win.

Nick arrived for this nighttime meeting and started off by calling Jesus "rabbi," which means "teacher." Now, there is no evidence that Jesus was considered a rabbi by anyone in the established religion in the area, so we can infer that Nick was being polite or shrewd, placing Jesus on his level, perhaps to throw Him off.

Nick then rightly noted that signs and wonders come only from God. If Jesus was truly performing these, it followed that

He must be on a mission from God. Of course, Nick didn't even get a question in before Jesus cut him off:

> Jesus answered him, "Truly, truly, I say to you, unless one is born again he cannot see the kingdom of God." (John 3:3)

The word translated "truly" in this verse is the word "amen." In the Old Testament, people often used "amen" at the beginning of a sentence almost like an upside-down exclamation point in Spanish. In the New Testament, the authors frequently threw it on the end of sentences to make an emphatic point.

Jesus was the only person in the New Testament who went old school and used it at the beginning of sentences, and He did it a lot. Throughout the gospel accounts, Jesus utilized this device about one hundred times to call attention to something important He was about to say.

In His conversation with Nick, Jesus doubled the emphasis by throwing down a "Truly, truly." Think of it like adding an annoying number of exclamation points to the end of a sentence when you're texting. What Jesus was about to say was that big of a deal. It was like He was saying ...

> Yo!!!! You have to get this!!!! Pay close attention!!!! Unless one is born again he cannot see the kingdom of God!!!! (John 3:3 Noel's Nonstandard Translation)

You must be born again. Amen, amen! Without being born again, you will never see the kingdom of God.

I don't know how many times I have heard people say, "I know you are a Christian, but are you born again?" And then there's the flip side: "I am a Christian, but not one of the *born-again* kinds."

Really? Seriously, there is no difference.

If you are a Christian, you are born again.

If you are born again, you are a Christian.

With Jesus repeating the "amen," it's a signal to us that what He says here is important enough that we better figure out what He's talking about. Luckily for us, Nick was just as confused as we are:

> Nicodemus said to him, "How can a man be born when he is old? Can he enter a second time into his mother's womb and be born?" (John 3:4)

Nick wasn't a dumb guy. He was pressing Jesus for an explanation by being sarcastic. In fact, his outburst definitely called for an *interrobang*.

An interro-what, you ask? Don't know what an interrobang is? It's this: ?. It's essentially the punctuation equivalent of "What the ...!?"

> Nicodemus says, "Born again? What the ...!?
> What am I supposed to do? Jump back into

my mom's uterus? What do I look like to you?"
(John 3:4 Noel's Nonstandard Translation)

Here was Jesus's explanation:

[Yo! Yo!!!!] I say to you, unless one is born of
water and the Spirit, he cannot enter the kingdom of God. That which is born of the flesh is
flesh, and that which is born of the Spirit is spirit.
Do not marvel that I said to you, "You must be
born again." (John 3:5–7)

Put yourself in Nick's sandals for a second. Jesus says, "Yo!
Yo!!!! You must be born again!" and because the mental image is
ridiculous, you say, "Born again? What the …!?" Then He says,
"Yo! Yo!!!! You need to be born of water and the Spirit. Why does
that freak you out? Of course you have to be born again!"

Jesus has just told you not to marvel at the truly marvelous,
so of course the only logical response is "?."

Jesus's phrase "unless one is born of water and the Spirit"
has caused two thousand years of "?s." There are lots of different
opinions about what Jesus meant here, but the important thing
is one must be spiritually born again.

The phrase "born again" has gotten a lot of abuse in our
culture, which is a shame, because it is such a powerful image. It
shows that you are new when you become a Christian, because
the old has passed away and the new has come. You're like a

newborn babe. The phrase also shows that you have life. It shows that there is a definitive moment when you pass from death to life. Before that moment, you were not a Christian; afterward, you are. A switch has been flipped.

Theologian Millard Erickson likens salvation to a two-sided coin:

> Conversion refers to the response of the human being to God's offer of salvation and approach to man. Regeneration is the other side of conversion. It is God's doing. In regeneration the soul is passive; in conversion, it is active.[1]

Lots of people like to fight about the timing of all of this. Which comes first: the chicken or the egg? The conversion or the regeneration? Here's my theological answer that will probably get me into a lot of trouble: I don't care. I'm not smart enough to know, and apparently neither was Charles Spurgeon, a famous preacher of the nineteenth century, who commented:

> Which is first, the new birth, or faith, or repentance? Nobody can tell which spoke of a wheel moves first; it moves as a whole. The moment the divine life comes into the heart, we believe: the moment we believe, the eternal life is there. We repent because we believe, and believe while we repent.[2]

At this point, you are probably getting lost in the theological mumbo jumbo. I'm getting lost just typing it. What does all of this have to do with anything?

Everything.

When you begin to follow Jesus, you are born again. In that moment, you are a new person. You have been converted. You have been regenerated. The wheel is spinning. There's a mystery to the whole thing. You may not realize all that is happening, but you certainly know that everything has changed.

> Therefore, if anyone is in Christ, he is a new cre-
> ation; the old has passed away, and see, the new
> has come! (2 Corinthians 5:17 CSB)

THE WONDER OF THE NEW BIRTH

One of the most important things I do as a pastor is steal babies.

Whenever a new mom and dad proudly (and tiredly) walk into the church with their new baby, I take it upon myself to steal the child. I pick her up and inspect her new little fingers and her new little eyes and her new little nose. It's all so fresh and new and wonderful.

You are new too, dear Christian.

Spiritually new.

You believed in Jesus, and He made you into something new. How that happened is a mystery. It's like a coin or a wheel or, as Jesus puts it, the wind.

> The wind blows where it wishes, and you hear
> its sound, but you do not know where it comes
> from or where it goes. So it is with everyone who
> is born of the Spirit. (John 3:8)

Jesus is making a fun play on words here. In fact, to the joy of fathers everywhere (mine first and foremost), He is making a pun. The word for Spirit is *pneuma*, and the word for wind is *pneuma*. It's as if He's saying, "The *pneuma* blows where it wishes, and so it is with everyone who is born of *pneuma*."

This is what salvation is like. How someone truly becomes a Christian and when it happens has a bit of wonder to it, which makes it even more special. Sometimes you can't tell exactly when the Spirit of God has moved in someone until you see things start to move in his life or you hear his world begin to rattle around.

Some people hear the gospel one time and *boom*, they get it. For others, it takes a lifetime. Nick, for example, was having a tough time with this:

> Nicodemus said to him, "How can these things
> be?" Jesus answered him, "Are you the teacher
> of Israel and yet you do not understand these
> things? Truly, truly, I say to you, we speak of
> what we know, and bear witness to what we
> have seen, but you do not receive our testimony.
> If I have told you earthly things and you do not

believe, how can you believe if I tell you heavenly things? No one has ascended into heaven except he who descended from heaven, the Son of Man. And as Moses lifted up the serpent in the wilderness, so must the Son of Man be lifted up, that whoever believes in him may have eternal life." (John 3:9–15)

Here was a brilliant, super-educated guy, and yet he just wasn't getting what Jesus was laying out there for him. He came to Jesus because a warning light was telling him something was going on with Jesus and His ministry. Except now he was realizing the warning light was his own.

So, Jesus said, "I know you want to understand the deep things, but you have to get the basics down first."

I have known a lot of brilliant people like Nick who want to fight about all the little details of Christianity when what they should really be concerned with are the basic truths about Jesus.

In the Greek and Roman culture of Jesus and Nick's day, there were all kinds of nonbiblical stories about humans who made it to heaven and were now able to give a report. Homer's *Odyssey* and Virgil's *Aeneid* are examples. Even today, people love to hear stories of alleged visits to heaven.

Jesus flipped this around and said, "Ignore all that stuff. Forget about people who say they went to heaven and came back. Deal with Me. I am here, and I came the other way— *from* heaven."

He then pulled out an old story that Nick would have known well but one that is not often taught in churches today. In this story, which you can find in Numbers 21, the children of Israel were complaining to God because He had rescued them from Egypt. (Yes, you read that correctly: they preferred slavery to rescue.) To punish them for their complaining, God sent serpents into their camp, and people were getting bitten and dying. They cried out to God to save them ("Oh, now you *want* to be rescued?"), and God had Moses make a serpent out of bronze and stick it on a pole in the middle of the camp. If anyone who was bitten looked up to the serpent to be healed, they would live.

Jesus was throwing a little foreshadowing at Nick. He was predicting that, one day, He Himself would be placed on a pole and anyone who looked to Him (and believed in Him) would live ... forever. They would go from death to life.

God wants life for people—eternal life. And because Jesus didn't want Nick to miss that point, He just laid it out there clearly for him:

> For God so loved the world, that he gave his only Son, that whoever believes in him should not perish but have eternal life. For God did not send his Son into the world to condemn the world, but in order that the world might be saved through him. Whoever believes in him is not condemned, but whoever does not believe is condemned already,

because he has not believed in the name of the
only Son of God. (John 3:16–18)

We all start out dead. But life can come, through belief in
Jesus. And this is not just a belief that He existed or still exists
(because even the demons know that, James 2:19), but it is placing your faith in His work on the cross, where He was lifted up
in the middle of the camp to save us. This is what it means to
be "born again."

And when it happens, the coin begins to flip in our lives, the
wheel begins to spin, and the wind begins to blow.

Jesus then wrapped up the conversation with an uncomfortable truth:

And this is the judgment: the light has come
into the world, and people loved the darkness
rather than the light because their works were
evil. For everyone who does wicked things hates
the light and does not come to the light, lest
his works should be exposed. But whoever does
what is true comes to the light, so that it may be
clearly seen that his works have been carried out
in God. (John 3:19–21)

Ow. We don't want this kind of talk from Him, do we? Since
we were dead, all of our deeds were dead. We still sin. Yes, okay,
okay, okay—we get it.

We don't like people to see our sin. We don't like people peering into our lives and exposing us for who we are, so we hide from the light like cockroaches rushing under the cabinets. How often have we seen celebrities and high-powered men and women hurry into hiding when the lights came on and they were caught in the middle of the kitchen floor?

I wonder if some secret in Nick's life was telling him that something was wrong. As a part of the religious elite, surely he of all people could get over any sin, right?

Jesus was saying to Nick (and to us), "Step into the light."

Now, if you do so, you may not like what you see. The deeds you thought were so great—all your "I'm okay because at least I ..." claims to external value—will very likely be exposed as "filthy rags" (Isaiah 64:6 KJV).

Salvation is like the wind. Good works are like the effects of the wind. A changed life is the result of the wind moving in our lives. God blows grace on us; we become born again; our lives begin to change.

Billy Graham once famously said:

> Can you see God? Have you ever seen Him? ... I've never seen the wind. I see the effects of the wind, but I've never seen the wind. There's a mystery to it.[3]

The effects of the wind.

This is like the Holy Spirit in our lives. When we have been reborn, there are effects in our lives.

Later on, some people were beginning to believe that maybe Jesus *was* the Christ, and a big division was happening over it. Even the guys who had been sent to arrest Jesus couldn't agree on whether to do it or not because of the controversy.

> The officers then came to the chief priests and Pharisees, who said to them, "Why did you not bring him?" The officers answered, "No one ever spoke like this man!" The Pharisees answered them, "Have you also been deceived? Have any of the authorities or the Pharisees believed in him? But this crowd that does not know the law is accursed." Nicodemus, who had gone to him before, and who was one of them, said to them, "Does our law judge a man without first giving him a hearing and learning what he does?" They replied, "Are you from Galilee too? Search and see that no prophet arises from Galilee." (John 7:45–52)

This is an incredible story. The Pharisees were slamming the officers (who were of a lower rank than them) and the people (of an even lower rank) for believing in Jesus. None of the Pharisees believed He was the Messiah. This wasn't just a couple of guys either; it was a huge room full of people all speaking in one voice.

Except one voice … Nick's.

He became the lone man who stood up for Jesus, saying, "Are we really going to judge Him without a fair trial?"

Then, later, when Joseph of Arimathea took Jesus's body down from the cross, you know who helped him?

Nick.

Nick was born again.

The grace of God transformed him relentlessly and radically.

CHAPTER 11

DRIP. DRIP. DRIP.
WHY IS GOD'S LOVE FEELING LEAKY AGAIN?

There is an insidious little bait and switch hidden inside how most Christians think about their faith. It's so subtle that most of us don't even notice we are doing it.

Our Christian walk starts out with a promise of a "free gift." We learn that salvation, arguably the greatest treasure under heaven or earth, has no strings attached.

But then, when we start thinking about how to actually live out our salvation—and this is so bizarre—we add a bunch of strings.

We say, "I am saved by faith, period," but then we tack on a whole set of things we think we must do to *stay* saved or, at least, to stay on God's good side. Attend church on the regular. Give a certain percentage of our income. Go to Bible study. Be in an accountability group. Serve at the church. Volunteer at the food pantry. Sing in the choir or worship band. Teach in VBS. String, string, string, string, string.

Or to use our metaphor of a leaky pan of God's love in our spiritual undercarriage: drip, drip, drip, drip, drip.

I can't help but wonder if we do all of this stuff because we want to *feel* like we are saved. The truth of the gospel slaps that sort of false theology right across its face.

A careful study of the New Testament shows that, whether you like it or not, you are becoming who you already are.

Yup, you read that correctly.

We have already explored how God is holy and we are not. We've drawn the natural conclusion that God saves us because we can't save ourselves. We've seen that even the faith we need to believe in Him is supplied for us (Ephesians 2:8). Like Nick, when we become born again, God's the one handling the entire workload. All of this means that we are right now exactly where we are supposed to be, no matter what any faulty sensor may be trying to tell us.

If all of this is true, why then do we think we have to do something to hold on to that salvation? As Paul writes, "O foolish Galatians! Who has bewitched you?" (Galatians 3:1).

SANCTIFICATION

Let me throw a churchy word at you: *sanctify*. It's the flip side of another word you are familiar with by now: *holy*. In fact, it comes from the same root word. Something that is holy has been sanctified, while something that is sanctified is holy. They both basically mean to be "set apart." (Remember the whole "cut away from the mass of normal" deal?)

God is set apart from us by His very nature. He's the only one in the story with a white hat. But God isn't the only thing that is cut away from the norm. In the Bible, many things are "sanctified" or "set apart":

- God sanctified (or set apart as special) the seventh day of creation for the purpose of rest (Genesis 2:3).
- God sanctified the temple for worship (2 Chronicles 7:16).
- God sanctified Mount Sinai to be His special place (Exodus 19:23).

Notice that God is *always* the one doing the sanctifying. A number of passages show God telling His people to sanctify things, but again, it's God calling the holy into being. The day, the temple, and the mountain did nothing to make themselves holy. They were acted on by God's "sanctifyinator." That means that, once God says they are sanctified, they are sanctified, and that is that.

It's the same with people … kinda. In the moment of our salvation, we are sanctified, and that is that. But in another sense, we aren't. God's love for us is sealed in permanently, and yet we still doubt it. We don't *feel* it all the time, even though it's not moved or changed or leaked.

Confused yet? This verse certainly won't help you at all:

> "We *have been sanctified* through the offering of the body of Jesus Christ once for all....
>
> For by a single offering he has perfected for all time those who *are being sanctified.*" (Hebrews 10:10, 14)

Wait … which is it? Have we been sanctified, or are we being sanctified?

Yes.

Gloriously, yes.

In other words, we are becoming who we already are. We are sanctified and we're becoming sanctified. We are holy and we're becoming holy. We have been set apart from the mass of the normal, and we are becoming set apart from the mass of the normal.

What's more, there is nothing we can do about it. Not that we'd want to!

You are being transformed by the relentless grace of God, whether you realize it or *feel* it or not. Because of this, you can quit trying to sanctify yourself and you can just live in light of this reality. God is taking care of it.

Sometimes we have difficulty believing all the things we have talked about in this book, especially the parts about God's love for us, because we don't *feel* perfect and we certainly don't act like it. We still struggle with sin. Every day. The faulty sensors are still there flashing their false warnings.

You know why that is? It's because we are still becoming who we already are.

Jesus's impetuous friend Peter (who, by the way, no one would ever pick to become a disciple ... except Jesus, of course) wrote a letter to a church that was so persecuted they were being scattered across the known world. To them, he said:

> Therefore, preparing your minds for action, and being sober-minded, set your hope fully on the grace that will be brought to you at the revelation of Jesus Christ. As obedient children, do not be conformed to the passions of your former ignorance, but as he who called you is holy, you also be holy in all your conduct, since it is written, "You shall be holy, for I am holy." And if you call on him as Father who judges impartially according to each one's deeds, conduct yourselves with fear throughout the time of your exile, knowing that you were ransomed from the futile ways inherited from your forefathers, not with perishable things

such as silver or gold, but with the precious blood
of Christ, like that of a lamb without blemish or
spot. (1 Peter 1:13–19)

I find it helpful to work backward as I examine certain Bible
passages like this one. So, let's give that a shot here.

"the precious blood of Christ, like that of a lamb without blemish or spot"

Jesus is the Lamb of God who was and is perfect, without blemish
or spot, whose blood was shed for us. Without Jesus, you don't
have Christianity. (Obvious, I know. Work with me.) Without the
shed blood of Jesus, you don't have Christianity. Our salvation—
all of it—centers on His work on the cross. This is our ransom,
which is better than *perishable things such as silver or gold.*

Notice Peter's reminder about the way they had tried to
get saved before they came to Christ. He said those ways were
"futile." Human effort is always futile … it's like digging a hole
on the beach when the tide is coming in.

But God has already taken care of this for us, through the death
of Jesus on the cross. This is the biggest of deals. My prayer for you
and me is that we would never take the work of Jesus on the cross
for granted, that we would see faulty sensors for what they are, and
that our lives would change. Not through human effort, because
that's futile, but because it has already been done for us.

The gospel should change everything about our lives. How
we see our spouses, how we do our jobs, how we parent our

children, how we vote, how we cook, how we drive [gulp], and how we mow our lawns.

I have one daughter and three sons. In a testosterone-laden house like that, there is a lot of clashing. When my kids were younger, it would drive me crazy, especially in the summer when they were home *all the time*. They had nowhere else to go.

To combat this, and in an effort to disciple our children when they were little, I posted some Bible verses on the fridge. One said, "Everyone should be quick to listen, slow to speak and slow to become angry" (James 1:19 NIV). Another said, "Why do you look at the speck of sawdust in your brother's eye and pay no attention to the plank in your own eye?" (Matthew 7:3 NIV). I put these on the refrigerator to show my boys how they should be living their lives. I fully expected those little squares of paper stuck on the appliance door to fix everything.

But nothing changed. I finally got so frustrated that I yelled, "What's your problem? Why don't you look at the refrigerator and read those verses?" They kept shouting at each other, and then I kept yelling at them. They were trying to explain their position, and I was telling them not to explain but to *read the stupid verses* and live that way because that's how you are supposed to live.

This went on for weeks. I got more and more frustrated and angry. Then one day I was mowing my lawn and thinking about my boys fighting, and suddenly I realized that *I* had been quick to anger. *I* had been quick to speak. *I* had been slow to listen. And I had been so concerned about the specks in my children's eyes that I hadn't seen the plank in my own eye.

This sin I had been committing toward my children, and the way I had not been parenting in a godly way, was one of the reasons Jesus went to the cross. He was nailed to the cross for the times I had been a bad parent to my children.

Well, that broke me. I pulled my children aside and repented and said, "All the things I was trying to call you to were not how I was living. Jesus has forgiven me—will you?"

Later the same week, I was reading the book *Because He Loves Me* by Elyse Fitzpatrick. I came across this passage, and it rocked me so much I felt she must've written these words just for me:

> One reason we don't grow in ordinary, grateful obedience as we should is that we've got amnesia; we've forgotten that we are cleansed from our sins. In other words, ongoing failure in our growth is the direct result of failing to remember God's love for us in the gospel. If we fail to remember our justification, redemption, and reconciliation, we'll struggle in our sanctification.[1]

What I was failing to do in my kids' lives, what I was failing to do in my own life, was to remember that I had been cleansed from my sins. Period. Full stop.

The truth about you and me is that we're cleansed, redeemed, and removed (cut off from normal) by Christ's redemption. God's love for you and me is sealed for all time inside an unbreakable space that contains both Him and us. Every doubt we have about this comes from the devil. Every message that says we're incomplete, pathetic, worthless, and destined to mess things up for ourselves and everyone else is a lie from Satan. Look at the truth and believe it, no matter what the dashboard lights are telling you. No matter what the bully on the playground is shouting in your ear.

"And if you call on him as Father who judges impartially according to each one's deeds, conduct yourselves with fear"
The price that was paid for us was so high that we must remember, if we call on God as Father who judges according to each one's deeds, to conduct ourselves with fear. We believe the false positives coming to us, and this is why a lot of Christians add the strings. We know we will one day stand before the judgment seat of Christ and He will judge how well we ran this race called life (Revelation 20:11–13). This has nothing to do with our salvation but everything to do with rewards in heaven. And so, we "conduct ourselves with fear." Why? Because God has said, "You shall be holy, for I am holy."

Remember, *holy* means "set apart." And Peter tells us where this will be seen: "you also be holy in all your conduct." We are to live lives that are *set apart* in conduct. That means there will be times when the world around us says to live one way and yet we determine to live another.

With God's words, He set us apart.

But do we act as if it's true? We talk with kids about peer pressure, for example, but adults aren't any better at standing up to it. In the workplace, where it's customary to pad your sales numbers, are you willing to be the lone person who is honest? When you are hanging out with the girlfriends and they are complaining about their husbands, are you willing to be the lone person who respects yours enough to speak well of him?

When you are at a party and everyone is having a few too many, are you willing to be the lone person who drinks moderately? When you are going out for the night, are you willing to be the lone person who dresses modestly? Are you willing to be set apart in your conduct?

This isn't something that comes naturally.

At the risk of sounding like there's a magical formula, Peter does give us a pretty good plan of how to be ready in these situations.

"preparing your minds for action"

Notice that this is something Peter is commanding us to do. Now, if I'd started with this bit, then when we finally got to salvation, it might seem that we are saved by something we do—by preparing our minds for action in a certain "saving" sort of way. That's why I went through the passage backward. I want you to see that this mind prep he's talking about has nothing to do with your salvation but is *based on* your salvation.

If you and I have been set apart as holy, and we have, then our response is to live a life that is set apart.

And it doesn't happen magically. It starts in our minds.

There is a great verse that says: "Don't copy the behavior and customs of this world, but let God transform you into a new person by *changing the way you think*. Then you will learn to know God's will for you, which is good and pleasing and perfect" (Romans 12:2 NLT).

How do we do this?

By the Word.

Jesus said it this way: "Sanctify them in the truth; your word is truth" (John 17:17).

I have often said that we live in a unique time and place in history when we have the advantage of having the Word of God in our language. But I think it can also be a disadvantage. We have forgotten how lucky we are.

Peter says we must have our minds prepared for action. What that means is that your mind has a challenge ahead. You are going to face situations in your life: work, school, parties, etc. And the question is whether you are going to be ready for action.

That's what the verses on our refrigerator did for me.

In baseball, we teach the kids to swing or throw in the same right way over and over and over until they have "muscle memory." Then, when something happens in a game, they react without thinking about it. It's the same with our minds. We train them in the right way until, in a difficult moment, we can react from memory. That's why Peter continues and says …

"being sober-minded"

This means being controlled from the inside, not from the outside. Circumstances, the people we are surrounded by, the websites we visit … they all exert control over us, moving us in a certain direction. Peter says to reverse that and be controlled from the inside by the Holy Spirit (and it is the Word that the Holy Spirit uses in our lives).

"set your hope fully on the grace that will be brought to you at the revelation of Jesus Christ"

The word "fully" means "unchangeably." We are to unchangeably lock our hope on Jesus, on the grace He has offered us, the grace that has saved us.

The context of much of 1 Peter is the fact that Jesus is coming back. Peter reminds his readers here that, when Jesus comes, that grace will fully grab hold of their lives. Until then, they are to set their minds on that reality, prepare their minds for action, and live from the inside out.

Does that mean we will always get better and better? Well, kind of …

Toward the end of his life, Gerhard Forde, an old Lutheran pastor, wrote these words:

> Am I making progress? If I am really honest, it seems to me that the question is odd, even a little ridiculous. As I get older and death draws nearer, it does not seem to get any easier. I get a little more impatient, a little more anxious about having perhaps missed what this life has to offer, a little slower, harder to move, a little more sedentary and set in my ways.… Am I making progress? Well, maybe

it *seems* as though I sin less, but that may only be because I'm getting tired! It's just too hard to keep indulging the lusts of youth. Is that sanctification? I would not think so! One should not, I expect, mistake encroaching senility for sanctification!

But can it be, perhaps, that it is precisely the unconditional gift of grace that helps me to see and admit all that? I hope so. The grace of God should lead us to see the truth about ourselves, and to gain a certain lucidity, a certain sense of humor, a certain down-to-earthness.[2]

The apostle Paul seemed to have had the same sort of thought process as he got older. The longer he was a Christ follower, the more deeply he realized what a sinner he was and how much he needed Jesus.

Many Christians are like this. If you talk with an older person who has been a Christian for a long, long time, what you will see is wisdom and knowledge and godliness, and what they will describe to you is a deeper need than ever for Jesus. The two go hand in hand.

One thing I don't see Peter proposing in his whole argument is that we should "focus on the now." When it comes to salvation, there's no need to focus on the now. The solution God wants you to give to the "now problem" is to fugetaboutit.

You have already been sanctified and you are being sanctified. It won't work to fixate on the faulty intel you're hearing in your mind. The key is to focus on the future and what Jesus did for you in the past.

People want a formula to fix their problems, but God gives us a person: Jesus. When we focus on Him, we grow. When we focus on ourselves, we don't. And when we focus on faulty sensors and false positives, we end up living as if they're true.

See, here's the problem. We tend to focus on the now. We tend to make our Christian life about our *feelings*, but that can really mess us up. We don't always feel full of God's love, but so what? Has God changed the arrangement? Or else we focus on our *actions*, and we become moralists who never feel like we are good enough, or we think we are superior to others. And to be honest, as author Steve Brown reminds us, that just makes us look ridiculous:

> If Jesus covered all your sins on the cross, you don't have to cover them.... When you try to cover your own sins (by being obedient or denying they're there) and be more righteous than God's own Son ... you're like a man who wears a bra. You're weird, you may like it, but it doesn't do you any good and has no practical purpose. Sorry.[3]

Focus on the truth, forget the false intel, stop trying so hard, and just live.

CHAPTER 12

JUST CHILL

JESUS WORKS SO YOU CAN REST

"What do you want from me?"

In unguarded moments, this question leaps from the trembling lips of spouses and teens, students and employees.

"Why does everyone want something from me?"

It seems like people are constantly reaching out their grubby paws for more: more affection, more performance, more points, more freebies, more tips, more sex, more time, more horsepower, more money … more, more, more, more, more!

Aren't Sundays supposed to be different? After a burdensome week filled with a cocktail of both perfectly reasonable and categorically unreasonable requests made upon you, you settle into an uncomfortable pew to sing some old songs and maybe get a moderate dose of encouragement to run the race for another week.

But then it happens again: The sermon is about what *God* wants from you. Read your Bible more. Forgive more. Love more. Give more. Volunteer more. Evangelize more. Get involved more. Come to church more. Serve more.

Will this parade of expectations never end?

One of my favorite movie scenes of all time comes from the underappreciated cinematic masterpiece *My Cousin Vinny.*

Attorney Vincent "Vinny" LaGuardia Gambini (brilliantly played by Joe Pesci) is cramming for his final arguments in the jury trial of his young cousin and his friend. While he hopelessly pores over a mountain of manila folders, law books, and legal pads, his fiancée, Mona Lisa Vito (played even more brilliantly by Marisa Tomei), stomps back and forth in front of him. Her sighs and the methodic *clump, clump, clump* of her boots finally break down his resolve, and he asks her what is going on.

She confesses that she is anxious about the trial because he had promised that, should he somehow win this case, the two of them would finally get married and start a family. She is worried, because the case does not seem to be going well. If Vinny loses this case and they don't get married, she is afraid they may never have kids.

Vinny's response to her reasonable (albeit inopportune) concerns is an echo of our response to God when He makes what seem like untimely and unreasonable demands on our lives:

Lisa, I don't need this. I swear to God, I do not need this right now, okay? I've got a judge that's just aching to throw me in jail. An idiot who wants to fight me for two hundred dollars. Slaughtered pigs. Giant loud whistles. I ain't slept in five days. I got no money, a dress code problem, and a little murder case which, in the balance, holds the lives of two innocent kids. Not to mention your biological clock, my career, your life, our marriage, and let me see, what else can we pile on … the top of the outcome of this case?[1]

Can you feel the avalanche rumbling just over his head? And don't we feel the same way sometimes, even at church? "Really, God? If You (or anyone else, for that matter) ask me for one. More. Thing …"

But what if we have God all wrong?

What if, despite what you have heard, God isn't asking for *anything* from you?

Sounds like a lie, doesn't it?

WHAT YOU REALLY NEED IS TOO BIG TO IMAGINE

The apostle Paul wrote out a prayer for a church filled with people he adored and yet who were on the verge of "losing heart" (Ephesians 3:13). You could say their warning lights were blinking. To combat their anxiety, Paul asked God to help them grapple with the enormity of His love for them, and the apostle closes his prayer with a profound theological truth:

> Now to him who is able to do far more abundantly than all that we ask or think, according to the power at work within us, to him be glory in the church and in Christ Jesus throughout all generations, forever and ever. Amen. (Ephesians 3:20–21)

It's nice and poetic and sounds pretty deep, but does it strike you? At one point, I knew the passage well enough that I didn't really see it anymore—until Ken Wuest's translation shook me up.

> Now to the One who is able to do beyond all things, *superabundantly beyond and over and above those things that we are asking for ourselves and considering,* in the measure of the power which is operative in us, to Him be the glory in the Church and in Christ Jesus into all the generations of the age of the ages. Amen. (Ephesians 3:20–21 WUEST)

Whoa.

God is able to do "superabundantly beyond and over and above" anything we can ask for.

- Superabundantly *beyond* all we can ask.
- Superabundantly *over* all we can ask.
- And superabundantly *above* all we can ask.

And it doesn't stop there. God is able to do superabundantly more than we can *consider*. That means you can't come up with a prayer request too big for God. You can't even scratch the surface of what He is able to do with your most creative imaginative powers!

Go ahead, mull it over and try to go big. In this moment—today—what do you *need*? What do you *want*?

In your relationships, your work, your life … where are the sticky spots? Where is the conflict? Where are the broken friendships that can never be repaired? Think. Imagine. Consider. Dream. Ponder. Ruminate.

And no matter how grand a list you come up with, God can do superabundantly more.

Now, I am the furthest thing from a prosperity gospel preacher, but maybe some truth has snuck into that false theology. If God is really as big as the Bible says He is, what could He do for you so that you are fully equipped to do the good works He's prepared for you to do? You and I can't wrap our puny little minds around the sheer possibilities.

So at the risk of assuming them impossible, let's consider what God really *could* offer us to fit us for service. God isn't a big ol' Santa Claus in the sky, but that doesn't mean He doesn't delight to give good gifts to His children.

WHAT YOU REALLY NEED IS TOO MUNDANE TO IMAGINE

Take a breath.

A big breath.

And listen to Jesus.

Jesus, who was accused of hanging out with prostitutes and (worse yet) IRS agents. Jesus, who was accused of drinking with drunkards and feasting with gluttons. And just when the accusations reached their most fevered pitch, He lifted His eyes to heaven and prayed to His Father. He thanked Him for the cluelessness of the so-called wise and the deep understanding of toddlers. He thanked God for the authority He had been given to exercise His supremacy on earth.

As He closed His prayer, I imagine that He looked into the weary eyes of the crowd, who probably couldn't help but wonder what He was going to ask of them.

Jesus took a deep breath, and I'm sure with tenderness in His eyes and gentleness in His voice, He spoke softly:

> Come to me, all who labor and are heavy laden, and I will give you rest. Take my yoke upon you, and learn from me, for I am gentle and lowly in heart, and you will find rest for your souls. (Matthew 11:28–29)

I will give you rest.

This may be really hard to believe, but Jesus doesn't want one more thing *from* you. He wants a lot *for* you. Sometimes all we see on the pages of Scripture is God desiring our worship, our service, our fidelity—and all of that is true. But none of it is the ultimate end. He desires these things for us because they are the fulfillment of what it means to be human. We were created for these things, and when we live in harmony with our ultimate purpose in Him, we flourish.

It all starts with *rest*. This is one of the greatest gifts He can offer you this side of eternity, because everything else flows from it. When you silence the false alerts going off in your life and you truly grasp that God has you right where He wants you, you can rest.

As I write this chapter, I am getting ready to take a sabbatical. In fact, I am writing this sentence as I am one hour away from telling our church staff that I am taking this break.

To be honest, I am terrified. I have been at this gig for twenty years and I am scared to stop striving. I was trying to get to the core of what I was afraid of when one of my copastors who coaches lots of people in ministry put his finger right on the spot. He told me that every pastor he has ever seen take a sabbatical is afraid or becomes afraid the first few weeks, and they all fear the same thing: irrelevance. They are afraid that people will grow so used to them being gone that they will no longer feel needed. They want to work hard, and to have people *see* them work hard, because that work gives them value.

But God says you have value apart from your work. You are valuable because you are His beloved child. You work from your value, not the other way around.

Jesus uses His limitless power and authority to give us what we desperately need: rest. That can be hard to believe with everything piling up all around us, can't it? Couldn't He use His power to pay our mortgage or tame the expectations of our mother-in-law? Nope. Not directly, anyway. In the midst of the crap we are surrounded by when we think, *I can't take one more thing*, Jesus says, "Come to Me. I will give you rest."

Rest is a gift, but we have a hard time seeing it that way. In our culture, with the old Puritan work ethic, we are told that good things come to those who work their tails off. We want good stuff (and lots of it), and we've always been told it will take some serious effort to get it.

It's definitely true to some degree. No Olympic athlete ever won gold without hard work. No concert musician ever succeeded without hard work. Our work must be done with excellence if we want to keep our jobs. Certainly, marriages and families require hard work too.

So it stands to reason that rest is something we should have to work hard to achieve, silly as that sounds. But rest *as a free gift from God* to His beloved is a theme threaded through Scripture.

The first pages of the Bible show us that, after God worked, He *rested* (Genesis 2:2). This rest became a pattern for the people of Israel (Exodus 20:8) and even the land itself (Leviticus 25:4). This rest was called "sabbath," which literally means "stop."

There's a lot to do. But you can stop. It'll be okay.

BE CHILL

In a psalm that is misquoted embarrassingly too often in the church, we are told to "be still, and know that I am God" (Psalm 46:10). The context of these words is a time of trouble, with the earth trembling and the mountains falling into the sea. The psalmist sings these words in the midst of nations raging and kingdoms toppling and the earth melting! In this world filled with devastation and wars, he calmly and softly sings, "Be still, and know that I am God."

That doesn't mean to sit in silence or get your daily quiet time on, though those are both fine things. It means to stop striving, to stop freaking out, and to stop trying to control everything. It means to stop paying attention to the faulty warning lights on your dashboard. You can *chill out* because God has it handled. He gives His people, especially on their worst days, rest.

Jesus has got this. He will not break a bruised reed or snuff out a smoldering wick (Matthew 12:20).

You can rest.

You don't deserve it. You can't strive for it. It's a gift of grace. Any voices to the contrary are not to be listened to.

Don't worry about what you are going to eat or how you are going to deal with that temperamental boss. You can chill, knowing that God's all over it.

> Seek first the kingdom of God and his righteousness, and all these things will be provided for you. Therefore don't worry about tomorrow, because tomorrow will worry about itself. Each day has enough trouble of its own. (Matthew 6:33–34 CSB)

Most of the time, we treat rest as a reward for work. But it isn't. Well, it actually is: *you* can rest because *Jesus* worked. So stop freaking out and just rest.

CHAPTER 13

LIVING WITH GOD, OTHERS, AND MYSELF

THE GLORIOUS NEW LIFE OF A WRETCHED SAINT

For this entire book, we have been talking about the beautiful and relentless grace of God. Why have I spent so much time on our need for grace and God's tireless desire to pour it out on us?

It's simple, really. The world needs you (and me) to not just *know about* God's grace but to experience it and let it get deep down in our bones. When that happens and we begin to believe the truth about ourselves—that we are beloved wretched saints—we can't help but begin to extend that grace to others. We can't help but begin to extend that grace to ourselves.

The key to dealing with the evil machinations of the sin engine this world runs on is graceful, wretched you. It's counterintuitive, but to be a light in this world (which is your calling, see Matthew 5:14), you are going to have to cut yourself some serious slack.

Many Christians I interact with don't offer themselves any of the grace God offers them. They see themselves as a wretch but not a saint.

In a valiant (but futile) effort to please God, they set an impossibly high bar for themselves, especially in their spiritual lives. They try to obey God's command to "be holy, because I am holy" (1 Peter 1:16 CSB) without realizing that, because of Jesus, they already are and that what they're hearing is a false report saying they have to prove their worth. Having been saved by grace, they try to perfect themselves by works (Galatians 3:2–3), and yet in doing so they nullify the grace of God (Galatians 2:21).

Sadly, many Christians shipwreck their faith by trying to take Jesus's job. Good luck with that! And usually, they end up undermining the message of the gospel to a watching world.

Maybe we need to approach Jesus like a little child might (Matthew 18:3).

A few weeks before writing this, I was sitting on the lovely stained concrete floor of our church lobby, holding an enthralling conversation with a little girl who was probably three years old. To be honest, I don't remember what we were talking about or how the conversation started. All I can remember was how, as she spoke, she ran her tiny little fingers through my beard. It wasn't that she was fascinated by my facial hair—in fact, she hardly seemed to be paying any attention to what she was doing. She was just ... well ... playing with my beard as she talked. I couldn't help but wonder if she had a cat or a dog at home and she was so used to petting it that her actions were more muscle memory than affection.

And this is not a onetime experience for me. I have had my beard tugged, caressed, and licked by little kids at my church. Yup. You read that right. One little boy licked my beard like an ice cream cone.

Contrary to the reaction I get from adults, my beard seems to be a comfort, a fascination, and a novelty all combed (ha, see what I did there?) into one for my youngest congregants. When teensy fingers touch my too-long beard, in some weird way I have never been able to figure out, I become a little more accessible to a young soul.

And when that happens, they tell me stuff. They feel safe.

I wonder if any little kids ever licked Jesus's beard. I'm guessing they did. Kids seemed to really love Jesus. Maybe it's because they knew He didn't want anything from them—He just wanted something *for* them.

The truth of the gospel of grace declares that the pressure is off. You can crawl up into the Father's lap and stroke (or lick) His beard and lay yourself bare, because He adores you and has taken care of everything, including your spiritual growth. You can almost see the smile on the apostle Paul's face as he prayed:

> I give thanks to my God for every remembrance of you, always praying with joy for all of you in my every prayer, because of your partnership in the gospel from the first day until now. I am sure of this, that he who started a good work in you will carry it on to completion until the day of Christ Jesus. Indeed, it is right for me to think this way about all of you, because I have you in my heart, and you are all partners with me in grace. (Philippians 1:3–7 CSB)

You are my partner in grace. All Christians are partners in grace together. God, who started a good work in you, *will* carry it on to completion until the day of Christ Jesus. It's a done deal, so cut yourself some slack, stop trying to top off a tank that isn't leaking, and bask in the grace.

What is that good work He *will* carry on to completion? Confirming you into the likeness of Jesus (Romans 8:29).

That includes making you a more grace-full person. In fact, the ultimate evidence that you are being conformed into Jesus's image is that you're showing more grace to others.

Because Jesus didn't just give His life *for* you; He gave His life *to* you. He took everything from you (your sin, your shame, your consequences), and He gave everything to you

(His righteousness, His inheritance, His relationship with the Father).

Martin Luther called this "the great exchange." Jesus took your sin and gave you His righteousness: "For our sake he made him to be sin who knew no sin, so that in him we might become the righteousness of God" (2 Corinthians 5:21).

This is the ultimate act of grace: you—a wretch—have become the righteousness of God.

It is who you are. You are a saint.

DAILY AFFIRMATION

There's a classic *Saturday Night Live* sketch in which Stuart Smalley (played by Al Franken, who later became a senator) would look at himself in the mirror and declare, "I'm good enough. I'm smart enough. And doggone it, people like me."

Maybe we need a daily affirmation too. I think it might go something like this: "I'm a wretch. I'm a saint. And doggone it, God loves me."

Once the faulty sensor has been silenced, those three realities will radically alter your interactions with God, with other people, and with yourself.

GOD

A memorable *Far Side* cartoon depicts God as a chef mixing together everything that will make up His creation. His ingredients include birds, insects, medium-skinned people, light-skinned people, dark-skinned people, reptiles, and trees. "And just to make things interesting," He adds a dash of *jerks*.

This image of God messing with His creation is baked into our collective psyche. For some, God is a tyrant intent on torturing humankind like a kid with a magnifying glass frying ants on the sidewalk. For others, He is a disinterested, absentee landlord who washed His hands of creation the moment He was done working on the sixth day. In between those two extremes are various caricatures that range from an abusive parent to a wise-cracking best friend (complete with a tuxedo T-shirt).

But the caricature fades away when we truly grasp that God is the all-powerful creator of the universe, who so adores wretched saints like us that He sent His Son, Jesus (John 3:16—there's that most famous phrase!), to face the same temptations we face, to live the life we cannot live, and to die the death we deserve (Hebrews 4:14–15). Armed with that conviction, we can walk boldly into His throne room (Hebrews 4:16), plop on the seat with our brother Jesus (Ephesians 2:6), and find all grace and mercy in our times of greatest need (Hebrews 4:16).

When our faulty sensor blares and Satan tries to condemn us, we can look at God the Father and know that He is looking back at us through Jesus (Colossians 3:3), and we can know we are okay.

In those moments when we are tempted to feel like we have to perform and we whisper to Jesus, "Get real with me, what do You want me to *do*? What are the *works of God* You want me to get busy with?" we can remember the answer He gave the crowd who asked Him the same question: "This is the work of God—that you believe in the one he has sent" (John 6:29 CSB).

OTHER PEOPLE

One of the greatest biblical pictures of a sensor going haywire is the Old Testament character Job. The Bible describes him as "blameless and upright, one who feared God and turned away from evil" (Job 1:1). You really can't get a better character reference than that. This dude even offered sacrifices to God for his kids' *possible* sins they may have committed when they partied (Job 1:4–5). Suffice it to say, the phrase "complete integrity" described him well.

Everything in Job's life was going along swimmingly—until in one instant, he lost it all. His wealth, his business, his family (with the exception of his wife ... we'll get back to her), and his health were suddenly gone. That's when the sensor started to blink.

As you can probably imagine, Job began to curse the day he was born (Job 3:1). His friends told him he must have done something to provoke God's wrath (Job 8:20), and his own wife told him to curse God and die (Job 2:9). The majority of the book of Job is a back-and-forth between Job and his friends as they try to diagnose why the sensor was going off.

The truth? There was nothing wrong. Was Job sinless? Nope. There was some stuff God had to correct him on and did so in epic form (Job 40–41), but it was all as it was meant to be, tragedy and all. When things were going great, no one questioned that God loved Job. When he had wealth and a Fortune 500 company and lots of kids, everything was just peachy. But when the sensor began to blink, everyone turned on Job. His friends had a moralistic view to his suffering: "If you had done right, you would be fine. So do right."

God spends His chunk of the conversation with Job's friends, who held an incorrect view of Him: "My anger burns against you and against your two friends, for you have not spoken of me what is right, as my servant Job has" (Job 42:7).

Imagine how this story would have played out differently if Job's friends had believed differently about God. What if they had seen the sensor for the false alarm it was? Instead of sanctimoniously declaring, "Do right," maybe they would have just kept doing what they had done at the start, when they showed up, sat down, and shut up (Job 2:12–13). Maybe they would have agreed with Job when he proclaimed, "The LORD gave, and the LORD has taken away; blessed be the name of the LORD" (Job 1:21).

I also can't help but wonder if Job's experience changed how he interacted with his friends, his wife, and his great-great-grandchildren (since God restored his fortune and family and allowed him to see them). When the false sensors began to blink in *their* lives, did Job show up, sit down, and shut up until they were ready to hear his story of God's love for the thousandth time? Because when you have believed God at your worst, when your thoughts and feelings have been informed by the truth, you will want to share it with anyone who will listen.

YOU

As I stand in front of my congregation to preach, I can't help but visualize thousands of blinking sensors. I know they are there because people tell me their stories. All the stories in this book are from real people, although I changed some of their names and combined some stories to protect their privacy. My assumption is that you picked up this book because, like with me and my congregation, you have something blinking on your dashboard. Someone—maybe it's Satan or your best friend or your own experience—is accusing you and telling you there is something wrong with you.

And I'm here to tell you that's a lie. Remember, when you believe something about yourself that is contrary to what God says is true about you, you can know your sensor is out of whack.

You are right where God wants you to be. He doesn't make mistakes and He doesn't miss a beat. I know you don't have your act together, but none of us do. Anyone who tells you differently wants to sell you something. I know it's a cliché, but the old bumper sticker is right: "Christians aren't perfect, just forgiven." Forgiven and loved and accepted and adored and right smack dab in the middle of God's plan.

Here's the truth that becomes astonishingly clear when the noise of the faulty sensors is finally put to rest:

Now we have this treasure in clay jars, so that this extraordinary power may be from God and not from us. We are afflicted in every way but not crushed; we are perplexed but not in despair; we are persecuted but not abandoned; we are struck down but not destroyed. We always carry the death of Jesus in our body, so that the life of Jesus may also be displayed in our body. For we who live are always being given over to death for Jesus's sake, so that Jesus's life may also be displayed in our mortal flesh. So then, death is at work in us, but life in you. (2 Corinthians 4:7–12 CSB)

The Bible is saying you are a wretched saint. You are a jar of clay (cheap and easily broken) and that makes you wretched. But as my friend Pastor Tyler St. Clair (of Cornerstone Church in Detroit) says, "There is a ruby, a diamond, inside the clay. The Lord has placed a priceless, powerful jewel—the gospel of Jesus Christ—in flawed, feeble humans." That makes you a saint!

Yeah, one day God will finish His work on the wretched part of us and show us how it was all part of the plan to make us a saint. But that day is (probably) not today. You can't rush it either. Jesus's good friend John (you know, the disciple whom Jesus loved) tells us as much:

Dear friends, we are God's children now, and what we will be has not yet been revealed. We

know that *when he appears, we will be like him*
because we will see him as he is. (1 John 3:2 CSB)

We won't be fully like Jesus until He is done working on us
and we see Him face to face.

Do you see the implication?

You get to be weak. You get to fail. You get to stumble. And
when things seem like they are breaking, it's because the clay
needs to fall away to show off the treasure inside. You are nothing more than a wretch and so much more than a saint.

That's the gospel truth.

ONE FINAL THING

The day after I turned in the final version of this book to my editor, my son called me on the phone.

"Dad … my check-engine light is on." And you are never going to believe what the problem was. Actually, there's a real good chance you know exactly what the problem was.

A faulty sensor. Classic.

I didn't know whether to laugh or cry.

I told my son he was going to be all right.

And you are too.

I've been at this whole following-Jesus thing long enough to know that the warning light on the dashboard of your life is going to light up again. And again, and again. The same old accusations, the same old lies, the same old fears are going to blink and blare again.

My prayer for you is that, the next time it happens, you will know what it is: a faulty sensor.

Emboldened by the love of God toward wretched saints like you and me, I pray that you will rip out that piece of junk sensor and inject a gob of grace into its place. When your feelings and thoughts drift from the truth of God's Word, I pray that you would have the strength to reject the lie, believe the truth, and just live.

And finally, I pray that as the lies drip away and the truth is all that remains, you would find the life abundantly that Jesus promised you.

Get on the road and just drive.

NOTES

CHAPTER 2: FAULTY SENSORS

1. Eliott C. McLaughlin, "Suspect Faces Felony Charge of Fatally 'Swatting' Man 1,400 Miles Away," CNN, January 4, 2018, www.cnn.com/2018/01/03 /us/kansas-police-shooting-swatting/index.html.

2. Shanika Gunaratna, "Study: Half of People 'Remember' Events That Never Happened," CBS News, December 9, 2016, www.cbsnews.com/news/half-of -people-remember-events-that-never-happened/.

3. Steven Reinberg, "Your Earliest Childhood Memories May Be False," CBS News, July 20, 2018, www.cbsnews.com/news/your-earliest-childhood -memories-maybe-false/.

4. Robby Berman, "Scientists Treat Anxiety by Implanting False Memories," Big Think, June 29, 2018, https://bigthink.com/robby-berman/scientists -treat-anxiety-by-implanting-false-memories.

CHAPTER 3: WRETCHED

1. "Amazing Grace" by John Newton (1779).

2. Michelle Kwan, Twitter, February 16, 2018, https://twitter.com/michellewkwan/status/964688460161343490.

3. George Whitefield, "Repentance and Conversion," in *Sermons on Important Subjects* (London: H. Fisher, 1841), 663.

4. Timothy Keller Sermon Archive (New York: Redeemer Presbyterian Church, 2013).

CHAPTER 4: JUST BELIEVE

1. Tim Challies, "I Feel, I Think, I Believe," Challies, February 22, 2016, www.challies.com/articles/i-feel-i-think-i-believe/.

2. J. D. Greear, Twitter, May 17, 2015, https://twitter.com/jdgreear/status/599960125022064640.

CHAPTER 5: HIGH STAKES LOST AND FOUND

1. Brennan Manning, *Ragamuffin Gospel* (Colorado Springs: Multnomah Books, 2005), 20.

CHAPTER 6: CHERISHED WHORE

1. "Victim Rachael Denhollander Confronts Nassar," CBS New York, YouTube, January 24, 2018, www.youtube.com/watch?v=-8jUCrPArHQ, time: 27:56–29:49.

CHAPTER 7: LOVING THE UNLOVABLE

1. Jefferson Bethke, *Jesus > Religion: Why He Is So Much Better Than Trying Harder, Doing More, and Being Good Enough* (Nashville, TN: Nelson Books, 2013), 7.

2. Paul F. M. Zahl, *Grace in Practice: A Theology of Everyday Life* (Grand Rapids, MI: Wm. B. Eerdmans, 2007), 36.

3. Timothy Keller Sermon Archive (New York: Redeemer Presbyterian Church, 2013).

4. Philip Yancey, *What's So Amazing about Grace?* (Grand Rapids, MI: Zondervan, 2008), 69–70.

CHAPTER 8: YET, HERE WE ARE

1. Alvin Plantinga, "Actualism and Possible Worlds," in *Theoria* (1976), 42:139–60, at Andrew M. Bailey, http://andrewmbailey.com/ap/Actualism _Possible_Worlds.pdf, accessed October 4, 2018.

2. Moses Y. Lee, "The Significance of the Korean Peace Summit: An American Civil War Analogy," Gospel Coalition, April 27, 2018, www.thegospelcoalition .org/article/the-significance-of-the-korean-peace-summit-an-american-civil-war -analogy/, forwarded by Harold Kim, Facebook, April 27, 2018, www.facebook .com/harold.kim.50/posts/10160272792150503.

3. Philip Yancey, *What's So Amazing about Grace?* (Grand Rapids, MI: Zondervan, 2008).

4. Philip Yancey, "Grace," 2009, https://philipyancey.com/q-and-a-topics/grace, accessed October 4, 2018.

5. *Selected Shorter Writings of Benjamin B. Warfield*, vol. 2, ed. John E. Meeter (Phillipsburg, NJ: Presbyterian & Reformed, 1970), 427.

6. John Stott, as quoted in Glenn E. Clifton, *The Glorious Grace of God Unveiled* (Nashville, TN: Westbow, 2017), Kindle location 7602.

7. Jerry Bridges, *The Discipline of Grace* (Colorado Springs: NavPress, 2008), 21–22.

8. Paul F. M. Zahl, *Two Thousand Years of Amazing Grace: The Story and Meaning of the Christian Faith* (Lanham, MD: Rowman & Littlefield, 2006), 7.

9. A. W. Tozer, *Knowledge of the Holy: Drawing Closer to God through His Attributes* (Zeeland, MI: Reformed Church Publications, 2018), 84.

10. *The New Sermons of Dwight Lyman Moody* (New York: Goodspeed, 1880), 95.

11. John Piper, *Future Grace: The Purifying Power of the Promises of God* (Colorado Springs: Multnomah Press, 1995), 73.

CHAPTER 9: GRACE-RICH GOSPEL THERAPY

1. Kerry Patterson, et al., *Crucial Conversations: Tools for Talking When Stakes Are High*, 2nd ed. (New York: McGraw-Hill, 2012).

2. Timothy Keller, Twitter, March 14, 2014, https://twitter.com/timkellernyc /status/444503440941907968?lang=en.

CHAPTER 10: BORN-AGAIN NICK

1. Paul Enns, *The Moody Handbook of Theology* (Chicago: Moody, 2014), 350.

2. *The Complete Works of C. H. Spurgeon*, vol. 31, sermons 1816–1876.

3. "Voice of [Billy] Graham from DC Talk's 'Mind's Eye' Song," posted by AnotherJesusFreak, YouTube, April 7, 2016, www.youtube.com/watch?reload =9&v=hYSgg3WvYeE.

CHAPTER 11: DRIP. DRIP. DRIP.

1. Elyse M. Fitzpatrick, *Because He Loves Me: How Christ Transforms Our Daily Life* (Wheaton, IL: Crossway, 2008), 44.

2. Gerhard O. Forde, *The Preached God: Proclamation in Word and Sacrament*, ed. Mark C. Mattes and Steven D. Paulson (Minneapolis: Fortress Press, 2017), 244.

3. Steve Brown, *Three Free Sins: God's Not Mad at You* (New York: Howard Books, 2012), 225.

CHAPTER 12: JUST CHILL

1. *My Cousin Vinny*, directed by Jonathan Lynn (Los Angeles: Twentieth Century Fox, 1992).

BIBLE CREDITS

IF JESUS HAS SET US FREE, WHY DON'T WE FEEL FREE?

Often, followers of Jesus feel more guilty instead of more free.

A powerful book for the spiritually restless, *Unchained* leads you to discover what it means to be set free. To be set free from religion and sin. Set free from shame and guilt. Set free to love, to live free, and to say yes to God's calling every day.

Understand—perhaps for the first time—what true freedom in Christ means.

noeljesse.com/books
Available everywhere books are sold.

transforming lives together